Discussions of
Shakespeare's Problem Comedies

DISCUSSIONS OF LITERATURE

General Editor JOSEPH H. SUMMERS, Washington University

DISCUSSIONS

OF

SHAKESPEARE'S PROBLEM COMEDIES

Edited with an Introduction by

Robert Ornstein

UNIVERSITY OF ILLINOIS

D. C. Heath and Company

BOSTON

CONTENTS

INTRODUCTION

ALTHOUGH the term "problem comedies" is an invention of modern criticism, *Troilus and Cressida, All's Well that Ends Well,* and *Measure for Measure* have been puzzling Shakespeareans for centuries. Dr. Johnson found Bertram, the eagerly pursued romantic "prize" of *All's Well,* an ungrateful wretch. Coleridge thought *Measure for Measure* the only painful play Shakespeare ever wrote and confessed that he did not know what kind of play *Troilus and Cressida* was or what to say about it. Hazlitt called *All's Well* one of Shakespeare's most pleasing comedies, but *Troilus and Cressida* seemed to him "loose and desultory" and the theme and characterizations of *Measure for Measure* such that "our sympathies are repulsed and defeated in all directions." Victorian critics commiserated with Troilus and admired Helena and Isabella, but in general they did not admire the problem comedies, which they found artistically unsatisfying as well as distasteful in theme, occasionally brilliant but often carelessly plotted and lacking in inspiration. Indeed, much of nineteenth-century criticism leaves the impression that these plays were works of the left hand, by-products of a period when Shakespeare's imaginative powers were absorbed in the great tragedies.

Armed with the findings of historical scholarship, twentieth-century criticism has been more rigorous in its approach to the problem comedies and, on the whole, more appreciative of their artistic qualities. A large number of fine, perceptive essays have made it unmistakably clear that these plays are too rich in poetic, moral, and intellectual substance to be dismissed as casual, or indifferently conceived, entertainments, or to be explained as products of a momentary depression and disillusion. Yet one might say that twentieth-century criticism has been more successful in defining the crucial issues of the problem comedies than in resolving them. For many modern essays are, in reality, little more than sophisticated restatements of earlier complaints and exasperations. Instead of objecting, as did earlier writers, to Shakespeare's choice of subject, modern critics will accuse him of mixing dramatic modes and genres, or of failing to unite the moral and satiric realism of his characterizations with the romantic conventions and artificialities of his *novella* plots. And though modern critics speak far more confidently than did Coleridge, the diametric clash of their opinions does not convince us that the last words have been written about the problem comedies, particularly when half a century of intensive critical commentary has failed to establish anything like common agreement about their tone, unity, or intention.

Of course controversy is not in itself unusual in the discussion of Shakespeare, but the long-continuing debate over the problem comedies is unique in that it seems to call in question our fondest assumptions about the clarity, nobility, or even humanity of Shakespeare's ethical perceptions. Although critics have argued passionately about Hamlet's psychological makeup or about his motives, they have rarely disagreed about the essential beauty and refinement of his moral nature. But when we turn from one discussion of *Measure for*

Measure to another, the characters assume radically different moral identities: white turns to black, the odor of sanctity becomes the stench of decay. Isabella, who is to one critic an angel of light, is to another a pitiless revelation of frigid virtue. Vincentio, who is to some critics a kind of earthly Providence, is to others a meddlesome Duke of dark corners. The clash of opinion over the characters in *Troilus and Cressida* and *All's Well* is less extreme, but it also suggests that the point of view in these plays is, if not ambivalent, certainly more difficult to ascertain than the point of view in *Twelfth Night* or *Macbeth.*]

The ability of the problem comedies to polarize critical opinion raises questions not only about the plays themselves but also about the theories and assumptions which underlie conflicting interpretations. For example, are the problem comedies ambiguous because of the failure of Shakespeare's art? Or are they deliberately and necessarily ambiguous because they deal with acts, motives, and dedications which are at once ideal and impure? Or do they *seem* ambiguous only because the aesthetic, ethical, and psychological assumptions of modern critics lead them to discover ironies and ambivalences which Shakespeare never intended? On the other hand, is there good reason to believe that Shakespeare's audience found the problem comedies less difficult and perplexing than we do? Does the appeal to convention erase the unpleasantness of the bed-tricks and of the endings of *All's Well* and *Measure for Measure?* Or does the appeal to convention eliminate the problems of the problem comedies by patronizing the Elizabethan mind and by ignoring the moral, intellectual, and psychological depths which Shakespeare lent to his source materials?

If the essays in this volume do not provide definitive answers to these questions, they do offer a wide variety of critical approaches ranging from the impressionism of Pater to the historical scholarship of Wilson, Leech, Bradbrook, and Dodds. Pater, Dowden, Quiller-Couch, Dodds, and Sewell focus, in different ways, on character; Traversi and Empson study verbal and poetic structure; Ellis-Fermor and Bradbrook discuss the artistic embodiment of theme; Spencer and Wilson, the relation of dramatic design to literary convention. Rather than excerpt selections from W. W. Lawrence's and E. M. W. Tillyard's books on the problem comedies, the editor has preferred to reprint less familiar and less easily accessible material. But the reader will find that Lawrence's and Tillyard's contributions are discussed at some length in several essays. He will also find in the essays references to many other valuable and important studies of the problem comedies which could not be included in this volume.

Without touching the extremes of dogmatism or special pleading, this collection illustrates the diversity of interpretations of the problem comedies in the past century and a half. In some instances the editor has underlined crucial points of disagreement and controversy by pitting one critic or critical position against another. But few of the essays are argumentative in themselves, though many of the authors take just a smack at those with whom they disagree. The emphasis falls upon the discussion of *Measure for Measure* because it is in many ways the most complex as well as the most controversial of the problem comedies, and because it has elicited an extraordinarily rich and varied critical response over the past century.

ROBERT ORNSTEIN

Discussions of
Shakespeare's Problem Comedies

Shakespeare's Problem Comedies

Samuel Taylor Coleridge

Troilus and Cressida

THE *Troilus and Cressida* of Shakespeare can scarcely be classed with his Greek and Roman *history* dramas; but it forms an intermediate link between the fictitious Greek and Roman histories, which we may call legendary dramas, and the proper ancient histories; *ex. gr.*, between the *Pericles* or *Titus Andronicus* and the *Coriolanus*, *Julius Caesar*, etc. *Cymbeline* is congener with *Pericles* distinguished from *Lear* by not having any declared prominent object. But where shall we class the *Timon of Athens?* Immediately below *Lear.* It is a *Lear* of the satirical drama, a *Lear* of domestic or ordinary life—a local eddy of passion on the high road of society, while all around are the week-day goings on of wind and weather—a *Lear*, therefore without its soul-scorching flashes, its ear-cleaving thunder-claps, its meteoric splendors, without the contagion and fearful sympathies of nature, the Fates, the Furies, the frenzied elements dancing in and out, now breaking thro' and scattering, now hand in hand with, the fierce or fantastic group of human passions, crimes, and anguishes, reeling on the unsteady ground in a wild harmony to the swell and sink of the earthquake.—But my present subject was *Troilus and Cressida;* and I suppose that, scarcely knowing what to say of it, I by a cunning of instinct ran off to subjects on which I should find it difficult not to say too much, tho' certain after all I should still leave the better part unsaid, and the gleaning for others richer than my own harvest. Indeed, there is none of Shakespeare's plays harder to characterize. The name and the remembrances connected with it prepare us for the representation of attachment no less faithful than fervent on the side of youth, and of sudden and shameless inconstancy on the part of the lady. And this, indeed, is the gold thread on which the scenes are strung, tho' often kept out of sight and out of mind by gems of greater value than itself. But as Shakespeare calls forth nothing from the mausoleum of history or the catacombs of tradition without giving or eliciting some permanent and general interest, brings forward no subject which he does not moralize or intellectualize, so here he has drawn in Cressida the portrait of a vehement *passion* that, having its true origin and proper cause in warmth of temperament, fastens on, rather than fixes to, some one object by liking and temporary preference:

> Fie, fie upon her!
> There's language in her eye, her cheek, her lip,
> Nay, her foot speaks; her wanton spirits look
>   out
> At every joint and motive of her body.

Reprinted by permission from *Coleridge's Shakespearean Criticism*, ed. T. M. Raysor (Cambridge, Mass.: Harvard University Press, 1930), I, 108–11.

This he has contrasted with the profound affection represented in Troilus, and alone worthy the name of love; affection, passionate indeed—swoln from the confluence of youthful instincts and youthful fancy, glowing in the radiance of hope newly risen, in short enlarged by the collective sympathies of nature—but still having a depth of calmer element in a will stronger than desire, more entire than choice, and which gives permanence to its own act by converting it into faith and duty. Hence with excellent judgement and with an excellence higher than mere judgement can give, at the close of the play, when Cressida has sunk into infamy below retrieval and beneath a hope, the same will, which had been the substance and the basis of his love, while the restless pleasures and passionate longings, like seawaves, had tossed but on its surface,—the same moral energy snatches him aloof from all neighborhood with her dishonor, from all lingering fondness and languishing regrets, while it rushes with him into other and nobler duties, and deepens the channel which his heroic brother's death had left empty for its collected flood. Yet another secondary and subordinate purpose he has interwoven with the two characters, that of opposing the inferior civilization but purer morals of the Trojans to the refinements, deep policy, but duplicity and sensual corruptions of the Greeks.

To all this, however, there is so little comparative projection given,—nay, the masterly group of Agamemnon, Nestor, Ulysses, and still more in advance, of Achilles, Ajax, and Thersites, so manifestly occupy the foreground that the subservience and vassalage of strength and animal courage to intellect and policy seem to be the lesson most often in our poet's view, and which he has taken little pains to connect with the former more interesting moral impersonated in the titular hero and heroine of the drama. But I am half inclined to believe that Shakespeare's main object, or shall I rather say, that his ruling impulse, was to translate the poetic heroes of paganism into the not less rude but more intellectually vigorous, more *featurely* warriors of Christian chivalry, to substantiate the distinct and graceful profiles or outlines of the Homeric epic into the flesh and blood of the romantic drama—in short to give a grand history-piece in the robust style of Albert Dürer.

The character of Thersites well deserves a more particular attention, as the Caliban of demagogues' life—the admirable portrait of intellectual power deserted by all grace, all moral principle, all not momentary purpose; just wise enough to detect the weak head, and fool enough to provoke the armed fist of his betters; whom malcontent Achilles can inveigle from malcontent Ajax, under the condition that he shall be called on to do nothing but to abuse and slander and that he shall be allowed to abuse as much and as purulently as he likes—that is, as [he] can; in short, a mule, quarrelsome by the original discord of its nature, a slave by tenure of his own baseness, made to bray and be brayed, to despise and be despicable.—Ay, sir, but say what you will, he is a devilish clever fellow, tho' the best friends will fall out; but there was a time when Ajax thought he deserved to have a statue of gold erected to him, and handsome Achilles, at the head of the Myrmidons, gave no little credit to his "friend, Thersites."

Frederick S. Boas

Troilus and Cressida

. . . Shakspere's lyrical period lay far behind him when he was attracted to the story of Troilus and Cressida. He saw in it the materials for a merciless satire of the high-flown ideal of love, fostered by the mediaeval cycle of romance, whence the tale had sprung. The absolute devotion of a gallant to his mistress, which this form of literature had glorified, is transformed into the delirious passion of a youth for a mere wanton. The knightly love which Spenser had sung of in *The Faerie Queene* as a sublime and half-unearthly rapture, the all-powerful stimulus to the practice of every virtue, is here exhibited as an intoxication of the senses, paralyzing the will, blinding the gaze, and sapping manhood at its source. Troilus, apart from his infatuation, is a model of youthful heroism. Ulysses, the critical observer, grows eloquent in his praise:

> The youngest son of Priam, a true knight:
> Not yet mature, yet matchless; firm of word,
> Speaking in deeds, and deedless in his tongue;
> Not soon provoked, nor being provoked, soon
>   calmed:
> His heart and hand both open and both free;
> For what he has, he gives; what thinks, he
>   shows;
> Yet gives he not till judgement guides his
>   bounty,
> Nor dignifies an impure thought with breath.
> Manly as Hector, but more dangerous.

Throughout the play he justifies this lofty tribute. He is foremost in the field, and if Pandarus is to be trusted, returns with his sword bloodied, and his helm more hacked than Hector's. In the council which debates the restoration of Helen as the price of peace, he displays a passion for glory which recalls Hotspur:

> Worthy Hector,
> She is a theme of honour and renown,
> A spur to valiant and magnanimous deeds,
> Whose present courage may beat down our foes,
> And fame, in time to come, canonize us:
> For, I presume, brave Hector would not lose
> So rich advantage of a promis'd glory,
> As smiles upon the forehead of this action
> For the wide world's revenue.

Yet this pattern of chivalry bemoans, in the paroxysm of his amorous frenzy, that he is

> Weaker than a woman's tear,
> Tamer than sleep, fonder than ignorance,
> Less valiant than the virgin in the night.

So hoodwinked is he by passion that he misreads the transparent characters of Pandarus and Cressida. In his eyes, and his alone,

> He's as tetchy to be woo'd to woo,
> As she is stubborn-chaste against all suit.

When at last he stands on the threshold of attainment, his brain reels in the dizzying vortex of his rapture:

> I am giddy: expectation whirls me round.
> The imaginary relish is so sweet
> That it enchants my sense. What will it be
> When that the watery palate tastes indeed
> Love's thrice-repured nectar? death, I fear me,
> Swounding destruction, or some joy too fine,
> Too subtle-potent, and too sharp in sweetness
> For the capacity of my ruder powers.
> I fear it much, and I do fear besides
> That I shall lose distinction in my joys;
> As doth a battle, when they charge on heaps
> The enemy flying.

Never has there been a more exact and subtle analysis of the delirious ecstasy that chokes in its own surfeit. And all this is for

Reprinted from *Shakspere and His Predecessors* (New York: Charles Scribner's Sons, 1908; first edition, 1896), pp. 373–84.

a shallow wanton in whom this heroic greenhorn, himself "as true as truth's simplicity," looks to find "a winnowed purity in love" equal to his own. He is ready to throw his glove to Death on behalf of her constancy, and if his heart flutters at her departure from Troy, it is only through dread that her faith should be corrupted by the insidious arts of Greek courtiers. When Ulysses leads him to Calchas' tent, and his own eyes and ears bear witness to the perjury of his idolized mistress, he seeks to discredit the evidence of his senses:

> This she? no; this is Diomed's Cressida.
> If beauty have a soul, this is not she.
> If souls guide vows, if vows be sanctimony,
> If sanctimony be the gods' delight,
> If there be rule in unity itself,
> This is not she.

But the bitter truth cannot be thus kept at bay, and Troilus is startled out of his callow optimism into a stern realization of the falsehood and wickedness of the world. His nature is however too sound for him to sit whimpering over his disenchantment. He seeks refuge from his heartache in strenuous achievement on the field of battle, and when we take leave of him, he is planning exploits of revenge for the death of Hector, whose fall has left him the foremost hope of Troy.

Shakspere's treatment of the story involves the degradation of Cressida. The charming coquette of Benoit, the voluptuous court-lady of Boccaccio, the tender-hearted widow of Chaucer, becomes in the play a scheming cold-blooded profligate. Such a woman does not need to have Troilus' suit pressed upon her by Pandarus, and if she "holds off" for a time, it is merely, as she frankly confesses, to gratify her vanity and eagerness for despotic sway over her lover:

> Women are angels, wooing:
> Things won are done, joy's soul lies in the doing.
> That she beloved knows nought, that knows not this:
> Men prize the thing ungained more than it is:

> That she was never yet, that ever knew
> Love got so sweet as when desire did sue.

This is not the language of passion, whether pure or unholy, but of that calculating wantonness which prefers the feeling of mastery even to sensual gratification. Yet when the confession of her partiality for Troilus cannot be any longer delayed, she cleverly poses as the deeply enamoured woman whose lips have hitherto been sealed by modesty. She affects a fear that, in her rapture, she will betray her emotion too unreservedly, and with an ambiguous request to stop her mouth, she draws him into kissing her. Then, with the artfulness of a consummate flirt, she pretends to be eager to hide her confusion in solitude, and can only be prevailed on to stay by a passionate declaration of Troilus' eternal fidelity. She protests her own unswerving loyalty with equal ardour, and crowns this mockery of genuine devotion by yielding to his wishes. When afterwards she hears that she is to be changed for Antenor, she declares that she will never leave Troilus, that she has forgotten her father, and that whatever extremes "time, force, and death" may do to her body, "the strong base and building" of her love

> Is as the very centre of the earth
> Drawing all things to it.

This expression, as Gervinus has noted, is ominous, and on her arrival in the Greek camp she at once shows herself in her true colours. She allows herself to be "kissed in general" by all the chiefs, and she gets the laugh of Menelaus by an equivocal jest. She does not gradually fall away from loyalty to Troilus, for of loyalty her shallow nature is incapable; she simply throws herself with redoubled zest into her old game in this new field. In Diomed, who has been her escort between the hostile lines, she spies, as she thinks, a fully qualified substitute for Troilus. But she has mistaken her man, and in the scene between the two in Act V, Shakspere has, with a few pungent strokes, delineated the Nemesis upon the heartless coquette. Diomed is no raw youth, dwelling in a fool's paradise, and seeing life through a rose-coloured haze. He is an experienced soldier and man of the world, who takes at a glance the measure of the woman with whom he has to deal. He "tames" her by a method as suited to her character and as effective as Petruchio's with Kate. When she tries on him her accustomed trick of holding off, instead of pleading for her favours, he taunts her with being forsworn, and turns his back upon her with a curt good-night. It is she then who, to keep him by her side, has to use entreaties and caresses, and even to offer him in pledge of her faith the sleeve given her by Troilus. The shallow coquette pays a heavy yet just price for her selfish levity, when she exchanges a chivalrous adorer for a harsh and imperious taskmaster. . . .

In the *Lucrece* Shakspere had introduced an elaborate description of the siege of Troy, and had there referred to Helen as "the strumpet that began this stir." The phrase gives us an important clue to Shakspere's motive for combining in one play the story of Troilus and Cressida and the broader theme of the conflict between Greece and Troy. Helen and Cressida are made to figure in exactly the same light. Both are heartless and disloyal, yet they awake a devotion of which they are utterly unworthy. The infatuation of Troilus is paralleled by that of Menelaus and Paris, whom Diomed cynically classes together as equally deserving of Helen:

> He merits well to have her, that doth seek her,
> Not making any scruple of her soilure,
> With such a hell of pain and world of charge.
> And you as well to keep her, that defend her,
> Not palating the taste of her dishonour,
> With such a costly loss of wealth and friends.

But Helen not only throws a spell over her individual lovers; she brings two nations into conflict for the sake of her *beaux yeux*. As Diomed asserts:

> For every false drop in her bawdy veins
> A Grecian's life hath sunk: for every scruple
> Of her contaminated carrion weight
> A Trojan hath been slain.

Hector makes a similar statement in the Trojan council when he urges the surrender of Helen as the price of peace. In his eyes "she is not worth what she doth cost the holding":

> 'Tis mad idolatry
> To make the service greater than the god,
> And the will dotes, that is inclinable
> To what infectiously itself affects
> Without some image of the affected merit.

These lines strike the very keynote of the play, and knit together the two plots. The "mad idolatry that makes the service greater than the god" is exemplified in the one on a personal, in the latter on a national scale. Troilus is infected by the mania as virulently in his public as in his private character. His rhapsodies over Cressida are not more glowing than over Helen, the

> Grecian queen, whose youth and freshness
> Wrinkles Apollo and makes stale the morning.

For her sake he, and, as is natural, Paris, are eager to risk the welfare of the entire Trojan state, and Hector, though he holds that "the moral laws of nature and of nation" demand her restoration, yields to the impetuous counsels of his younger brothers, and confesses that he has already sent a 'roisting challenge' among the Greeks. The debate moves throughout in the circle, not of antique, but of mediaeval ideas. It illustrates and implicitly condemns the quixotic sacrifice of great national interests to a fantastic code of exaggerated gallantry. . . .

As Pandarus inflames the passion of Troilus by depreciating the charms of all the Trojan ladies except Cressida, so Patroclus flatters Achilles' infatuated self-esteem by parodying all the other Grecian commanders. Ajax is similarly infected; he bears his head as proudly as Achilles,

Keeps his tent like him,
Makes factious feasts: rails on our state of war,
Bold as an oracle, and sets Thersites
To match us in comparisons with dirt.

This diseased self-love, an exaggeration of Hotspur's passion for honour, blinds the judgement no less than the diseased sentimentality of Troilus. The two commanders scorn every element of warfare save the brute strength in which they personally excel; the finer strategy which taxes the brain they sneeringly dub "bed-work, mappery, closet-war." How disastrous this factious arrogance is to the main enterprise is made clear by Hector's challenge. Achilles would be the natural champion of the Greeks in the duel with the foremost warrior of Troy, and in Nestor's eyes it is essential for him to take the field, as the result of this combat will influence the entire campaign. But Ulysses demurs:

What glory our Achilles shares from Hector,
Were he not proud, we all should wear with
    him,
But he already is too insolent;
And we were better parch in Afric sun
Than in the pride and salt scorn of his eyes.

It will therefore be wiser to choose the Greek champion by lot, and to arrange that it shall fall to Ajax. This will give an opportunity for exalting the latter above Achilles, and thus "physicking the great Myrmidon who broils in loud applause." To yet further "physic" him, the adroit Ulysses devises the incident of the Greek chieftains passing their haughty colleague as he stands at the door of his tent, with curt, disdainful greeting. Ulysses himself brings up the rear, and interprets to him the effects of his scornful withdrawal from the fray. He demonstrates that abilities, however pre-eminent, are practically nonexistent, unless they are exercised on the general behalf and receive their recognition in the grateful applause of the multitude:

That man, how dearly ever parted,
How much in having, or without, or in,
Cannot make boast to have that which he hath,

Nor feels not what he owes, but by reflection;
As when his virtues shining upon others
Heat them, and they retort that heat again
To the first giver.

Achilles' arrogant self-idolatry has thus a suicidal effect on his glory, and it has allowed Ajax to supplant him in the eyes of mankind, which fixes its gaze solely on present achievements. Ulysses thus plays the reverse role to Pandarus. The latter uses his knowledge of the world, in the lowest sense, to inflame the delirious passion of Troilus. Ulysses uses his far loftier experience of men and things to cure the self-love of Achilles. But his exhortations have little effect. A letter from Polyxena is enough to keep Achilles still back from the fray, and he is only roused to action by the death of Patroclus at the hand of Hector. Careless as ever of the general interest, he seeks no foe but the slayer of his friend. At their first meeting, Hector, with overstrained chivalry, forbears to strike because Achilles is fatigued: at their second it is the Trojan who is at the disadvantage, but generosity has no place in the Grecian's breast; he hounds on his Myrmidons against his defenceless enemy, and when he is dead drags him brutally at his horse's tail. Thus the scene closes in an atmosphere of squalid atrocity. With truth it has been said that in this play "we are introduced to heroic personages in order to be cured for ever of hero-worship."

But whatever rag of nobility still clings to the chief actors in the drama is pitilessly stripped off by Thersites, who to some of his original Homeric characteristics, now adds those of the Shaksperean fool. The result is a loathsome creation, who has enough of coarse plebeian insight to spy out all that is bestial beneath the fair shows of human life, and enough licence of speech to vent the leprous scum of his brain where he will, with nothing worse to fear than a cudgelling. . . .

Whatever Thersites touches he leaves polluted with slime. Mankind as viewed by him does not belie the description of it in

Gulliver's Travels as "the most pernicious race of little odious vermin that Nature ever suffered to crawl upon the face of the earth." And indeed the spirit in which Shakspere conceived the character of Thersites is akin to that in which Swift drew the appalling picture of the Yahoos. Not that this nauseating figure is to be taken as the "chorus" of the play. His profanation of all things human is as far removed from the sane, equitable worldly wisdom of Ulysses as are the delirium of Troilus, the self-love of Achilles. They are dazzled to realities by the false glitter of fantastic ideals; Thersites is blinded to them by a congenital disease of moral vision. But only in a mood of bitterest disenchantment with the world could such a character have been conceived. Even were he removed, the atmosphere of the play would still be black with the shadow of a great eclipse. And in this case the flight of time has added to, instead of, as often, taking away from the effect of the work. The reader of to-day mourns the degradation of the mediaeval romance of love and chivalry into a satire, however legitimate in itself, of the mediaeval ideals. It is turning the swords of the offspring against their mother's breast. And even if this be pardoned, we shudder, as an Elizabethan would never have done, at the spectacle of the god-like creations of the Greek Muse being dragged through the dirt. It scarcely soothes our pain, though it rectifies our judgement, when we realize that the Achilles of Shakspere is not "the Great Achilles whom we knew," that his Ajax is simply a *magni nominis umbra.* They are mediaeval figures decked out in borrowed trappings, and the shafts that riddle them glance harmless from the glorious forms under whose titles they masquerade. But even as a satire of chivalry, *Troilus and Cressida* overshoots the mark. The feudal code of love and honour, artificial though it be, deserves better than to be made the butt of savage scorn. Cervantes, within almost the same hour, had discovered a more excellent fashion of smiling it away.

D. A. Traversi

Troilus and Cressida

THE close relationship between the values of love and war, which is one of the most marked features of *Troilus and Cressida*, corresponds to a conception of dramatic unity which, although its antecedents can be traced respectively to the sonnets and the historical plays, was, at the time of writing, new in his work. The novelty consists in uniting, in a manner mutually illuminating, a personal theme and its public, "social" extension. Instead of a political conflict objectively studied and commented on by a character (such as Falstaff) who stands, in a sense, outside it, we are presented with a personal issue—the story of two lovers of opposed parties—set in the context of the Trojan war. The situation of the lovers is variously connected with the cleavage between the warring parties to which they respectively belong; and the connection thus dramatically established is further strengthened by the pervasive presence of imagery which suggests disruptive tendencies barely contained within a common way of feeling. The result, in terms of poetic drama, is less a finished and coherent creation than a statement of emotional ambiguity, the reflection of an experience deprived of order and seeking clarification through its own expression.

The nature of this ambiguity, and more particularly its relation to the preoccupation with time, which we have already considered in the sonnets, is perhaps best studied in the passage in which Troilus takes leave of Cressida:

CRESSIDA:

And is it true that I must go from Troy? . . .
        Is it possible?

TROILUS:

And suddenly; where injury of chance
Puts back leave-taking, justles roughly by
All time of pause, rudely beguiles our lips
Of all rejoindure, forcibly prevents
Our lock'd embrasures, strangles our dear vows
Even in the birth of our own labouring breath;
We two, that with so many thousand sighs
Did buy each other, must poorly sell ourselves
With the rude brevity and discharge of one.
Injurious time now with a robber's haste
Crams his rich thievery up, he knows not how;
As many farewells as be stars in heaven,
With distinct breath and consign'd kisses to
    them,
He fumbles up into a loose adieu,
And scants us with a single famish'd kiss,
Distasted with the salt of broken tears.
                  (IV, iv)

The verbal intricacy of this speech is highly characteristic of the play and helps to throw light upon the peculiar nature of its inspiration. The experience it reflects is, verbally at least, tremendously rich, endlessly elaborate, but the ordering of it is not equal to the complexity. The adverse action of time upon the parting lovers is represented by an astonishing number of verbs—"puts back," "justles roughly by," "rudely beguiles," "forcibly prevents," "strangles"—but the emotion does not *develop*, does not acquire added coherence in the course of its expression. It remains a long and acutely sensed effort to express a single moment of conflicting feeling. It belongs, in short, to a period in Shakespeare's development in which the keenness of his apprehension of certain elements of experience (already for the most part indicated in the sonnets) was not accompanied by a corresponding sense of

Reprinted from *An Approach to Shakespeare*, second revised edition (Anchor Books, 1956), pp. 63–81; used by permission of Sands & Co., Ltd. First published in 1938.

order and significance. We shall see that order and significance gradually growing out of the increasing mastery of his art.

Nonetheless, though unsatisfactory, the experience behind *Troilus* is highly individual. In each of the verbs of parting which we have just collected there is an element, sharply and vividly realized, of harsh and hostile physical contact. This laboured feeling is balanced by the poignant thinness of the positive love imagery which so inadequately accompanies it. Troilus, whose awareness of separation is so acute, so tangibly conceived, can only express his passion in images as intense as they are airy and essentially bodiless. Love is indeed "rich" in his estimation, fit to be mentioned with the "stars in heaven"; but it can only be expressed in "sighs" and "labouring *breath*," in the hurried breathlessness of "distinct *breath* and consign'd kisses," and in the intensely palated but transitory delicacy of "Distasted with the salt of broken tears." Opposed to this "airy," pathetic passion, the full brunt of the senses is felt in every phrase that stresses parting. "Rudely," "roughly," "forcibly," time and hostile circumstance undermine the tragic brevity of love, so that the "lock'd embrasures" which should normally convey the intensity of physical union are felt to be only an effort to snatch a moment's identity in the face of events which are forcibly drawing the lovers apart. The parting imposed by external circumstances, indeed, is subsidiary to a certain weakness inherent in passion itself. The ideal, which is perfect union, is desired intensely, but is as light as "breath" or "air"; and the bodies through whose coming together alone this intensity can be enjoyed are always, while they are united, "labouring" against a tendency to separate. Their "labour," irrevocably frustrated, issues in nothing tangible or permanent. Throughout *Troilus* the elements in love making for separation are too strong for those which desire union, and "injurious time" is the process by which

separation is born out of desired consummation.

Troilus and Cressida, then, in so far as it deals with the central pair of lovers, projects a metaphysical situation into the evocation of a personal relationship. The play is, in this as in other respects, the product of a profound uncertainty about the value of experience. The personal consequence of this uncertainty, as it affects more particularly the love poetry of Troilus, is the corruption of romantic sentiment. This is apparent in his first account of Cressida:

> I tell thee I am mad
> In Cressid's love; thou answer'st "she is fair";
> Pour'st in the open ulcer of my heart
> Her eyes, her hair, her cheek, her gait, her voice,
> Handlest in thy discourse, O that her hand,
> In whose comparison all whites are ink
> Writing their own reproach, to whose soft seizure
> The cygnet's down is harsh, and spirit of sense
> Hard as the palm of ploughman.   (I, i)

The underlying convention here is clearly Petrarchan, romantically abstracted from common reality. It makes itself felt in the assertion that Troilus is "mad" for love, in the strained use of "pour'st" and "handlest" to describe Pandarus's speech, in the comparison of Cressida's hand to the "cygnet's down," and in the introduction of "ink" to bring out by contrast its superlative whiteness. But the conventional imagery is transformed, as it were, from within in a manner so closely bound up with the convention that it acts as a corrupting agent, intimately related to the surface sentiment. By giving deep sensuous value to the Petrarchan images, it conveys simultaneously an impression of intense feeling and an underlying lack of content. "Handlest in thy discourse" is, as I have said, a far-fetched, literary image; but it brings with it a notable keenness of touch which is developed in the contrast between harshness and the "soft seizure" of the cygnet's down and in the almost un-

natural immediacy of "spirit of sense."
Yet the conventional note remains, and
with it the feeling that Troilus's passion,
for all its surface intensity, has an inade-
quate foundation, is vitiated by the strained
self-pity which allows him to refer to "the
open ulcer of my heart," and by the weakness to which he confesses in the course of
the same speech: "I am weaker than a
woman's tear."

It is important to realize why this weakness, which Cressida shares with her lover,
does not produce a tragedy of character,
but of situation. The tragedy indeed consists less in the personal suffering of the
lovers than in the overriding influence exercised by time upon all human relationships and feelings. In *Antony and Cleopatra*, at least while the lovers are united by
their feeling for one another, personal
emotion has become strong enough to
override mutability; in *Troilus*, the su-
premacy of time is never really questioned,
and so a consistent status as persons inevitably eludes the lovers. Their weakness
reflects the uncertainty of mood in which
the play was conceived and to which they
owe the peculiar poignancy, more than
sentimental and less than tragic, with
which they meet their personal fortunes.
Antony and Cleopatra, as lovers, are fully
drawn human beings because their love,
while it lasts and within its own clearly
defined limitations, is valid and confers
upon their emotions a full personal value.
Conversely, the complete realization in evil
of Regan and Goneril in *King Lear*, with
the sensual ferocity that characterizes it,
proves that when he wrote that play, Shakespeare felt himself able to distinguish between the various elements in his moral
experience without falling into ambiguity
and confusion. Antony and Cleopatra, Regan and Goneril have full reality as characters precisely because they proceed from
a clear understanding in their creator of
the value of human emotion as distinct
from the evil possibilities contained in it.
Troilus and Cressida, however, with its

intuition of passion as vain and transitory,
is compatible with no such individuality
of presentation; for time, as it is under-
stood in this play, destroys personal values
and makes them invalid.

This limiting observation can be applied
with equal force to the behaviour of both
lovers, and through the entire action. Cressida's falseness does not spring from a
deep-seated perversity or even from a strong
positive attraction for Diomed, but from
the mere process of events, from a flaw inherent in the human situation. Her tragedy, such as it is, derives from awareness
of her helplessness. We feel it in her pathetic appeal when Troilus prepares to
leave her after the night they have spent
together:

> Prithee, tarry;
> You men will never tarry,   (IV, ii)

and in the moment of self-knowledge in
which she tells him:

> I have a kind of self resides with you,
> But an unkind self that itself will leave
> To be another's fool.   (III, ii)

There is something in the expression of
this uncertainty, half punning and conventional, which makes it difficult to conceive of Cressida as a fully realized being.
At most she lives for us only in the mood
of the moment, with barely a sign of that
responsibility and consistency which is involved in the very conception of character.
Any attempt to subject her inconsistency
to a moral, of the kind which the mediaeval
elaborators of this legend had in mind
when they denounced her "faithlessness,"
is out of place because the spirit in which
Shakespeare created her made it impossible
for her to be shown as really responsible
for her actions; and without responsibility
there can be no moral evaluation. When
she comments in the early part of the play
on her refusal to reveal her feelings for
Troilus:

> Yet hold I off. Women are angels, wooing;
> Things won are done; joy's soul lies in the do-
>   ing,   (I, ii)

her aphoristic lines are not a revelation of wantonness, but simply an impression of the sense, which constitutes the only true tragedy of this play, of the impossibility, the meaninglessness of constancy in a world where time dominates human relationships and where attraction and separation seem necessary and connected aspects of a single situation.

This impossibility also dominates the poetry of Troilus himself and is there further developed from its original basis in romantic sentiment. Troilus's passion, even before it is faced with the necessity for separation, is strong only in anticipation. The intensity of its sensations is conveyed in a refinement of physical feeling, in an attempt to embody in terms of the senses an insubstantial and incorporeal emotion:

> I am giddy; expectation whirls me round.
> The imaginary relish is so sweet
> That it enchants my sense; what will it be,
> When that the watery palates taste indeed
> Love's thrice-repured nectar? death, I fear me,
> Swounding destruction, or some joy too fine,
> Too subtle-potent, tuned too sharp in sweetness,
> For the capacity of my ruder powers:
> I fear it much, and I do fear besides
> That I shall lose distinction in my joys. . . .
> (III, ii)

The sensations of this passage are intense enough, but only on the palate and through the senses; like the corresponding emotions of Cressida, they scarcely involve any full personality in the speaker. Troilus's emotions are concentrated on "expectation," on "the *imaginary* relish," and he feels that the "watery palates" will be too weak to sustain the actual consummation. The whole speech turns upon this contrast between the refined intensity of feeling which he seeks, self-consciously and with a touch of indulgence, in "Love's *thrice-repured* nectar," and the giddiness, the "swounding destruction," which would follow its impossible consummation. The experience of love, it is suggested, is so fine, so "subtle-potent," that it surpasses the

"ruder powers" of the body and remains an incorporeal aspiration which the senses strive vainly to attain.

Yet, by a strange contradiction, it is precisely because fulfilment in love is sought by Troilus exclusively on the sensual level that it proves unattainable. We can see now why the poetry of this play makes such extensive use of the imagery of taste, why Cressida, for example, says, before she leaves Troy for the Greek camp:

> The grief is fine, full, perfect, that I taste.
> (IV, iv)

Taste is a sense at once luxurious, delicate, and transitory; also it can be connected, in gross opposition to Troilus's bodiless idealism, with digestion and the functioning of the body. For the weakness of Troilus's passion, as we have already suggested, implies that it is patent of corruption; and that corruption—it can now be added—is the logical consequence of an effort to extract from the refinement of the sensual a substitute for spiritual experience. Immediately before the speech just quoted there is a striking turn of phrase in his appeal to Pandarus:

> O, be thou my Charon,
> And give me swift transportance to those fields
> Where I may *wallow* in the lily-beds
> Proposed for the deserver. (III, ii)

The ideal aspirations of Troilus remain abstract, intangible; such intensity as they achieve derives from their subjection to time, from their awareness of their own transitory nature. But this impermanence makes them bodiless, so that the sensual instincts, unable to associate themselves fully with the insubstantial ideal of union in a mutual passion, express themselves both weakly and basely, "wallowing" in what would be, if it were more forceful, a corrupt satisfaction.

This special use of the contrasted implications of sensual experience is extended in the course of the play from the personal to the public action, and contributes thus to the unity of its conception. The refined imagery of taste given to the Trojans, and especially to Troilus, reflects a bodiless ideal which becomes, in the mouths of the scurrilous Thersites and the Greek cynics, a series of clogged, heavy references to the digestive processes. Thersites has "majestic jaws," and Achilles calls him "my cheese, my digestion," while Agamemnon tells Patroclus that Achilles's virtues

> like fair fruit in an unwholesome dish
> Are like to rot untasted.   (II, iii)

In fact, the very sense which expresses the related intensity and lightness of Trojan passion becomes, in the Greeks, a symbol of inaction and distemper out of which issue the boils, "the botchy core," of Thersites's disgust.

In this way we pass from the individual to the public action, from the love of Troilus and Cressida to the war between the Greeks and Troy. This connection between the private and the public theme is indeed the most original feature of the play. The two parties, like the two lovers, are divergent within a common type of feeling. The Trojans share the fragile intensity of Troilus. They are deeply concerned with the value of "honour" and with a view of love which aspires to be idealistic, while Hector shows the virtues of war which are so noticeably absent from the bulky Ajax and the graceless Achilles. Typical of them is the speech in which Troilus explains the case for continuing the war:

> But, worthy Hector,
> She is a theme of honour and renown;
> A spur to valiant and magnanimous deeds,
> Whose present courage may beat down our foes,
> And fame in time to come canonize us.
>   (II, ii)

Yet the lightness and grace of this idealism covers a certain artificiality. It reads, at this stage in Shakespeare's development, like a survival from earlier plays set against the contortions and involutions of so much of *Troilus*. The impression is neither accidental nor isolated. Hector's reasoning in the same scene shows clearly that the arguments advanced by Troilus are as flimsy in content as their expression is tenuous. For all this "honour," for which Troilus is ready to fight and, if need be, to die, is directed to the defence of Helen, whose worth has been destroyed by the manner in which she has been stolen from Menelaus. Even Paris can only plead that he

> would have the *soil* of her *fair* rape
> Wiped off in honourable keeping her,

and Troilus, conveying a slight but unmistakable twist to conventional imagery, declares that Paris

> bought a Grecian queen, whose youth and *freshness*
> Wrinkles Apollo's and *makes stale* the morning.

The juxtaposition of "fair" and "soil," "freshness" and "stale," touches the basic weakness of Trojan idealism, and points to the way in which that idealism is organically connected in its expression with the sluggish inertia that prevails in the Greek camp.

The true nature of this Trojan weakness is perhaps most explicitly stated by Troilus when he sets forth, in an attempt at reasoned expression, his argument for the continuation of the war:

> I take to-day a wife, and my election
> Is led on in the conduct of my will;
> My will enkindled by mine eyes and ears,
> Two traded pilots 'twixt the dangerous shores
> Of will and judgement: how may I avoid,
> Although my will distaste what it elected,
> The wife I chose? There can be no evasion
> To blench from this, and to stand firm by honour.
>   (II, ii)

Troilus's terminology is indefinite and the expression of his argument, like so much of what passes for discussion in this play, far more complicated than its content. There seems at one point to be an opposition of "will," which we may associate here with sensual impulse, and "judgement," by which this impulse should normally be restrained and directed; the opposition, in short, of sensuality and moral control, which became a little later the central theme of *Measure for Measure*. In that play, however, the moral conflict is explicitly stated, and—what is more important—takes shape in a dramatic clash of clearly defined personalities; in *Troilus and Cressida* there is only an uncertainty, a sense of uneasiness, which the notable incoherence of the expression reflects. The conclusion reached by "judgement" is that affirmed by Hector—"value dwells not in particular will," but rather in a weighing of alternatives in the light of the principles of reason—but the whole trend of Troilus's reply is to annihilate, or at least confuse, the distinction between "will" and "judgement" themselves, to show that "judgement" is powerless and irrelevant once the sensual will has impelled man towards action. In other words, the basis of Troilus's "honour" is simply sensual impulse, and its weakness lies largely in his unwillingness to recognize this fact, and in the abstraction and lack of content which follow in the train of this evasion.

Hector, indeed, is sufficiently outspoken on the subject of Troilus's infatuation:

> Is your blood
> So madly hot that no discourse of reason,
> Nor fear of bad success in a bad cause
> Can qualify the same? (II, ii)

The argument—though Troilus rejects it and Hector himself fails to follow it to its conclusion—once more binds the personal love theme to that of the justification of public action. Troilus—and in this he is typical of the Trojans—refuses to admit the weakness of his conception of honour, which is, however, implied in the very situation which brought the war into being: for the reality of Helen, as Hector points out, does not correspond to Troilus's embroidered and Marlovian conception of her:

> Brother, she is not worth what she doth cost
> The holding. (II, ii)

But this same lack of solid foundation is apparent, as we have seen, in the undertones of Troilus's own poetry, where the unacknowledged sensual basis of his idealism refuses to be entirely suppressed. Underlying the "poetical" quality of Troilus's emotional flights, there is a distinct strain of coarseness and inertia. It appears in the references, so typical of this play, to the "soiled silks" and the "remainder viands" which are thrown away "because we now are full." Most typical of all, in the determination to hide its own weakness which it implies, is the Trojan reaction to reason:

> Nay, if we talk of reason,
> Let's shut our gates, and sleep: manhood and honour
> Should have hare hearts, would they but *fat* their thoughts
> With this *crammed* reason: reason and respect
> Make *livers pale* and lustihood deject.
> (II, ii)

This insistence upon mental inertia and the obstruction of physical processes, as applied to reason, stands in significant contrast to the lightness and artificiality of Troilus's idealistic outbursts, but they are organically related to them. The Trojan devotion to honour, Shakespeare would seem to infer, is devotion to an abstraction that has no sufficient basis in reason, that is, in fact, no more than an empty justification of impulse; but—it is equally important to realize—to abandon honour for its lack of rational foundation is to expose oneself to the danger of lethargy, to a rooted disinclination to act at all.[1] Once more we are faced with the split between motive and impulse, moral *value* and sensual substitutes, which dominates this play, without a real glimpse of resolution.

The analysis of this important scene suggests how the contrast between the Greek and Trojan parties, which most crit-

[1] The relation of this to *Hamlet,* and in particular to such a soliloquy as "How all occasions do inform against me" (IV, iv) is worth careful consideration.

ics have noted, is modified by significant points of contact. The Trojans, for all their concern to defend honour against the Greeks, are strangely related to their enemies. This relationship, of course, is openly "symbolized" in the combat between Hector and Ajax (IV, v), when Hector refuses to carry on the duel with his "cousin-german" and Ajax agrees to call a truce. But the contacts established through a common type of imagery are still more important for an understanding of the play. Where the Trojans reject reason in favour of ill-considered action, the Greeks accept it and are reduced to inaction. Agamemnon's very first speech, as the head and cornerstone of Greek unity, shows how inconclusive are the intellectual processes so painfully followed by the leaders who accompany him and how closely related they are to the views expressed by Troilus on "crammed reason":

> Princes,
> What grief hath set the jaundice on your cheeks?
> The ample proposition that hope makes
> In all designs begun on earth below
> Fails in the promised largeness; checks and disasters
> Grow in the veins of actions highest reared,
> As knots, by the conflux of meeting sap,
> Infect the sound pine and divert his grain
> Tortive and errant from his course of growth.
> Nor, princes, is it matter new to us
> That we come short of our suppose so far
> That after seven years' siege yet Troy walls stand;
> Sith every action that hath gone before,
> Whereof we have record, trial did draw
> Bias and thwart, not answering the aim
> And that unbodied figure of the thought
> That gave it surmised shape.   (I, iii)

Agamemnon's thought proceeds not from point to point according to a definite logical sequence, but by a series of indeterminate digressions which illustrate his incapacity to come to a conclusion. His laboured illustrations destroy the coherence of an argument which they do nothing to further; as so often in this play, there is no recognizable development of thought to justify the complexity. The repeated doublings of words—"checks and disasters," "tortive and errant," "bias and thwart"— all lay emphasis upon obstruction, upon the speaker's struggle against obscure impediments which hinder the Greeks from successful action; and the use of unusual and unassimilated Latinized words, such as "conflux" and "tortive," produces a similar sense of resistance and difficulty. More significantly still, these obstructions are associated with disturbances and interruptions in organic growth. The prospect of hope "fails in the promised largeness," does not grow to its anticipated stature. "Checks and disasters" are intertwined with natural growth, and the very rising of the sap in the "sound pine," which is so eminently a natural process, produces infection and distortion in the growth of the tree. Most important of all, because corresponding to the spirit expressed by Troilus, thought is "unbodied" and its processes, separated from the actual course of events, are equally cut off from the sensual immediacy which finds irresponsible expression in the comments of Thersites. The keen nervous quality so noticeably lacking in the theoretical observations of the Greek leaders breaks out significantly in Thersites's sweeping affirmation of anarchy and disorder; in a similar manner, Troilus's disembodied idealism covers a sensual impulse which he refuses to recognize.

It is only natural that this discrepancy in the Greeks between thought and action should be expressed in terms of physical disorder; and here the link with the Trojans becomes even more explicit. Thersites's boils and plague-spots are related to Agamemnon's laborious thoughts on authority just as Troilus's contempt for "crammed reason" and his insistent sense of soilure and physical obstruction are connected with his abstract idealism. The vital point in Shakespeare's presentation of the Greeks is this association of continual ratiocination with a complete overthrow of "degree"; they are entirely unable to turn council into united action. The position in the Greek camp is briefly summed up by Thersites: "Agamemnon is a fool to offer to command Achilles; Achilles is a fool to be commanded of Agamemnon; Thersites is a fool to serve such a fool; and Patroclus is a fool positive" (II, iii). While Agamemnon, Nestor, and Ulysses scheme and discuss, Ajax and Achilles "fust" out of action; the hand that executes is out of touch with the "*still and mental* parts" that contrive the conduct of the war. Perhaps the point is most clearly made by Ulysses in his account of Achilles's pride:

> imagined worth
> Holds in his blood such swoln and hot discourse
> That '*twixt his mental and his active parts*
> Kingdom'd Achilles in commotion rages
> And batters down himself.   (II, iii)

The conflict in Achilles between personal pride and duty to the Greek cause is stated here in terms of "blood," of sensual passion; the implications of "swoln and hot," suggesting feverish disorder due to extreme intemperance, are unmistakable. The adjective "kingdom'd," like so many of the words which characterize the poetry of this play, is not fully explicit, but it clearly refers the personal issue back to the general theme of "degree." The individual warrior, like the Greek polity at war, should be a unity founded upon "degree"; and "degree" in the individual is an ideal correspondence between thought and action, impulse and control, "blood" and "judgement."[2]

On both sides this balance is profoundly disturbed. The "cunning" of the Greek leaders is manifestly out of touch with practical considerations and expends itself in

an activity completely disproportionate to the desired end: "it will not in circumvention deliver a fly from a spider, without drawing their massy irons and cutting the web" (II, iii). On the Trojan side the infidelity of Cressida finally undermines Troilus's faith in "honour" as a basis for action and leaves him dimly aware of the incompatible and contrary elements which underlie what he had assumed to be the indivisible simplicity of passion:

> Within my soul there doth conduce a fight
> Of this strange nature, that a thing inseparate
> Divides more wider than the sky and earth;
> And yet the spacious breadth of this division
> Admits no orifex for a point as subtle
> As Ariadne's broken woof to enter.
> Instance, O instance! strong as Pluto's gates;
> Cressid is mine, tied with the bonds of heaven:
> Instance, O instance! strong as heaven itself,
> The bonds of heaven are slipp'd, dissolved and loosed:
> And with another knot, five-finger-tied,
> The fragments of her faith, orts of her love,
> The fragments, scraps, the bits and greasy relics
> Of her o'er-eaten faith, are bound to Diomed.
>   (V, ii)

All the characteristics of the love poetry of Troilus can be recognized here—its tenuous and unnaturally refined expression, its subtlety in dealing with distinctions within an apparent unity, its sensuous thinness balanced by the imagery of disgust and repletion which connects it with the verse given to the Greeks and indicates the unifying factor in this play. For the ambiguous attitude towards experience which so deeply exercised Shakespeare in many of his sonnets is the determining factor in his presentation of both parties. Proceeding from his sense of the disharmony introduced by their subjection to the temporal process into the love of Troilus and Cressida, it extends to embrace the two parties in their fantastic and unreasonable conflict. The Trojans follow a false idealism, which deceives itself with talk of "honour," but is really based on "blood" and ends in a pathetic and helpless realization of its own

[2] Compare *Hamlet*:
> . . . blest are those
> Whose blood and judgement are so well commingled
> That they are not a pipe for fortune's finger
> To sound what stop she pleases.   (III, ii)

insufficiency; the Greeks elaborate endlessly a "judgement" that is out of touch with the instinctive sources of action, until Agamemnon's chaotic reasoning finds its proper counterpart in the distorted bitterness of Thersites's diseased sensibility.

The fundamental impulse of this play, and the link which binds personal cleavage to political disorder, is now clear. Ulysses's argument on "degree" reduces itself finally to an intuition of self-consuming passion:

> Then everything includes itself in power,
> Power into will, will into *appetite*;
> And appetite, an universal wolf,
> So doubly seconded with will and power,
> Must make perforce an universal prey,
> And last eat up himself.   (I, iii)

The speech is saved from the charge of abstraction by this relation of "degree" to the disorder introduced by passion or "appetite" into the human organism. This disorder, present on both sides in the conflict between Greeks and Trojans, is the real theme of the play. The Trojans seek to ignore the limitations of passion in a bodiless idealism; the Greeks, quite incapable of idealism, are weighed down by all that the Trojans try to forget. Both sides are bound together by the occasion of their quarrel; as Thersites says: "All the argument is a cuckold and a whore." Troilus, in one magnificent phrase, sums up the crux from which the varied contradictions of the play draw their interest:

> This is the monstruosity in love, lady, that the will is infinite and the execution confined, that the desire is boundless and the act a slave to limit.   (III, ii)

The infinity sought by the will is the idealistic love of Troilus, which neglects the wearing action of time and the related inability of passion to live up to ideals of love and honour which can only be redeemed from abstraction by an adequate spiritual integration; and the very boundlessness of the desire, when it encounters the limits imposed by time and the body to which, in the absence of such an integration, it feels enslaved, turns to the clogged inertia of Achilles and the endless self-scrutiny of the Greek camp.

Una Ellis-Fermor

"Discord in the Spheres": The Universe of *Troilus and Cressida*

THE great play of *Troilus and Cressida*, one of the most weighty in the Jacobean period, has had a strange fate. Its readers have been variously affected by it, and our reflections, when we have not taken refuge in silence, have ranged from dismissing it as a piece of hasty work to defending it as a failure on a grand scale. Commentators [1] describe, in the one case, the ill-digested scenes mixed with graver, sometimes noble, matter, and in the other point out that, though Shakespeare had undoubtedly something which he wished to say (and to say in specifically dramatic terms), he for once mistook "what may be digested in a play," and, by sheer pressure of content, broke the mould he tried to use.

By repeated readings of the play, helped greatly by seeing it upon the stage, by trying to relate it to the criticism of life offered by some of Shakespeare's Jacobean contemporaries (to say nothing of the criticism of life implicit in some of our own contemporaries), I am driven to believe that this is not enough; that the play of *Troilus and Cressida* is not a great failure to record a phase of experience beyond the scope of dramatic form, but a great achievement, perhaps one of the greatest, in the expression of that phase, transcending those limitations to produce a living work of art.[2] That the actual experience which is thus expressed is of deep significance to our generation I no more doubt than that it is essential to our understanding of Shakespeare's later tragic and constructive plays; but for the generations between Shakespeare's and our own it has been generally avoidable, and therefore rare. It is no light matter to suggest that something in any way important to our understanding of the play should have escaped a long succession of commentators. Nor would anyone venture upon doing so today, were it not that our actual experience of disintegration and disruption, so unlike that of any age between, has thrown fresh light upon the nature and foundations of what we call civilization; prospects once mercifully rare are now common and familiar, and much that has not, in the interval, been generally forced upon the imagination, now lies upon the common road for every man's necessary consideration.

The great plays that follow this one in psychological sequence,[3] *Timon of Athens*

---

[1] These, ranging from Coleridge in the early nineteenth century to Professor F. S. Boas in our own time, with the addition of the quite recent work of Professor Wilson Knight and W. W. Lawrence, however widely they differ otherwise, agree in remarking in some way upon the contradictions in mood and assessments of values to be found in the play.

[2] I was for many years satisfied to see in this play a momentary failure of Shakespeare's artistic power. The failure was, on the contrary, in my understanding. It would be well, no doubt, if every critic were to hang upon the wall of his workroom the timely admonition: " 'Tis not Homer nods but we that sleep."

[3] It is the psychological sequence rather than the chronological that mainly concerns us here. It is undoubtedly possible for a mature artist to produce works in an order which does not precisely represent the order of the phases through which his mind is progressing at that time. This is made clear in the cases of some later artists who have left, in letters and journals, a complementary record of their thought and experience.

Reprinted from *The Frontiers of Drama*, third edition (London, 1948; first edition, 1945), by permission of Methuen & Co., Ltd.

and *King Lear,* are expressions of a further phase of the same experience; disintegration is accomplished, "Nature's germens tumble all together, Even till destruction sicken" and the judgement surrenders. In the moment of surrender the mind perceives another dimension of reality, and this perception leads in the end to the positive, spiritual revaluation in the last plays. But *Troilus and Cressida* stands at a lower point of negation in this sequence than *Lear* or even *Timon.* For, while its material is still that of the actual world, the mood is that of a man who has come to the end of that world's resources; emotional, intellectual, and moral values resolve alike into futility; even the imagination, the high constructive power, looking ahead into a dark night of the soul, sees no further ideal form, no "unbodied figure of the thought" waiting upon creation. This last experience is an area of suffering peculiar to the artist's mind, but it can derive from an experience potentially common to all men, the vision of the disjunction and disintegration of civilization—the ideals it rests upon and the achievements it bequeaths—while these are still co-extensive for him with the universe of thought. It is, in fact, in this very image that Shakespeare chooses to embody his experience in this play. What is recorded in *Troilus and Cressida* is thus the acutest point of suffering in this sequence, before the understanding has surrendered its moral, intellectual, or imagina-

The letters of Ibsen, taken in conjunction with his plays, are, of course, one of the most familiar examples of this kind of record, showing this kind of variation, in modern dramatic art. With the Jacobean playwrights many factors, even including professional demands, would be at work, but more important than these would still be those revivals and recrudescences of earlier moods which often characterize the apparent irregularities of spiritual growth. It is for this reason that we may discover some of the relations between Shakespeare's plays more clearly by considering them in what we believe to be their psychological sequence rather than in what we conjecture to be their chronological.

tive synthesis and accepted disintegration; the fullest possible realization of imminent dissolution before its accomplishment brings anaesthesia.

Readers of drama often receive piecemeal the experience of which a play is the record, looking first at individual parts or aspects of it; indeed, it requires either the highest imaginative capacity or prolonged knowledge to receive so complex and so vast an artistic experience as is communicated by a great play. Let us concede to this habit for the moment, if only because it will take us by the shortest road to some essential truths about *Troilus and Cressida,* the consideration of various single aspects being a kind of preliminary exercise before we attempt to receive the communication of the artistic experience.

In *Troilus and Cressida* the aspect we are first aware of is, as in many plays, the material of which it is made. For the artist this has meant the choosing, from the infinite and unselected mass of life, of those groups of characters and events to which his mind turns for the purposes of its as yet undefined interpretation; it is the first step in the substitution of the form of art for the chaos of life. For the reader it means the subject-matter of the play and his general impression derived from it; the series of characters, the chronological sequence of events, the impinging of character and event upon each other. And in *Troilus and Cressida* this takes the form of a succession of violently contrasted characters, events, and sentiments. Characters as discordant as Thersites and Troilus, Nestor and Pandarus, Hector and Cressida, Agamemnon and Achilles are forced into continual and jarring contrast, with no attempt to resolve the contradictions in an enveloping mood of humour or pity. Instead, the nucleus of the character-grouping, upon which our attention is continually focussed as in a well-composed picture, is that of Troilus and Cressida; a serious man, by nature heroic and an honest if confused idealist, and a light woman, equally by nature a

> sluttish spoil of opportunity
> And daughter of the game.

The same pitiless enforcing of contrasts is seen in the relation of character and event, the incompatibility of men's endeavours and their destinies; the ideal love of Troilus and the betrayal it meets at the height of its glory; the honourable, heroic code of Aeneas and Diomede, Hector and Agamemnon, and the collapse of that code in Achilles' murder of Hector; the clear, sustained thought of the debates upon principles and policy in the Greek and Trojan council chambers, and the relapse into petty feuds and ambushes, which serves to show how far that noble sanity can work upon event. And as we watch these passions, ideas, and achievements annihilate each other with no promise of compensation or solution, we fall more and more into agreement with Thersites, the showman who is ever at hand to point the futility, the progressive cancelling out to negation.

The materials of *Troilus and Cressida* are thus more obviously at war than those of any other play of Shakespeare's, and their discord has been a main factor in persuading its readers of the unevenness of the play, of the inconsistency in quality and treatment of the different parts, attributable, it might be, to indifference or weariness in the writer or to alternating and unreconciled moods of admiration on the one hand and expostulation, disgust, or disillusionment upon the other.

But what if this effect be itself art? What if disharmony be, not the result of a photographic reproduction of materials that the artist's mind has registered without full comprehension, but a deliberate commentary? For, significant and familiar as is the bitterness, the loathing of life which brought together the elements of *Troilus and Cressida*, the apposing of these is even more notable than the choosing. That aspect of a play which its readers think of as its form is itself a mode of interpretation of the material, having been for the artist the next step in the freeing of "that unbodied figure of the thought, That gave it surmised shape." The elements fall into such positions or relations within the scheme of his play as not only emphasize and disengage the nature and quality of each, but indicate the underlying values by which his interpretation of the material was determined.

This is revealed first and most obviously in the sequence of the scenes, and here the effect is best appreciated in a rapid production which preserves the Elizabethan tempo and forces us to see one scene running as it were into the next; by insisting upon their almost merging in presentation, it makes clear to us that they must be merged also in our interpretation; that they are, in fact, inseparable. Thersites or Pandarus (the explicit or the implicit statement of the mood of disillusionment) breaks in upon every scene in which nobility of conception, passion, or conduct is emphasized, following it up, almost before the echoes of the last words have died away. The induction and the conclusion are in the hands of Pandarus. Pandarus's talk precedes the great council-chamber scene in the Greek camp, where Ulysses builds his lofty image of the state; and Nestor and Ulysses (two of the wisest figures of the play) are hardly off the stage before the scurrilous venom of Thersites is poured upon them in the next scene. Straight upon this comes the corresponding council debate in Troy, with its penetrating analysis of one of the fundamentals of the play, the nature of value; and straight upon that again, Thersites calling up vengeance, "or, rather, the Neapolitan bone-ache," upon both armies. Into this meeting of Thersites and Patroclus come again the Greek leaders, their lofty statesmanship tinged now perforce with politic cunning, and upon that again the scene (III, i) between Pandarus, Paris, and Hel-

en; the feverish frivolity of the background
of the war jars bitterly with the scenes of
camp and battle and yet is inextricably interwoven with them. Straight upon their
urbane and matter-of-fact jesting upon the
habit of love, come Troilus's ideal, tremu-
lous anticipations, and into this very scene
again, Pandarus, that "wondrous necessary
man." This handling continues all through
the play, but the sifting together of the elements becomes closer and closer as it goes
on; Pandarus is nearly always present with
Troilus and Cressida in Troy, and Thersites
takes his place in the scene of Troilus's
disillusionment in the Greek camp. The
highest altitudes of chivalry are touched in
the scene of Hector's visit to Agamemnon,
where a noble code makes possible this
courteous friendship between honourable
enemies. The scene is set between that
which sees Cressida "wide unclasp the table
of her thoughts To every ticklish reader"
and that in which Thersites denounces Patroclus's relations with Achilles. This does
not seem like accident.

There is something, then, in the form of
this play which leads us to believe in its
unity of intention. Moreover, the belief that
it is not inconsequent and contradictory
but intent and purposeful, is confirmed by
our first experience of the imagery and the
prosody. The tough resilience of the verbal
music, the explosive illumination of the
imagery are the marks of a causal, not a
casual, direction. The speeches of Ulysses,
Agamemnon, Hector, and Nestor are distinguished by close-woven, intricate, and
virile imagery, and the ring of the verse
throughout these scenes is superb. When
Ulysses persuades the Greek councillors, he
gives a noble smoothness and simplicity of
line to his doctrine of hierarchical "degree." When Nestor is alone with Ulysses,
a mind thewed like his own, he speaks with
cryptic cogency a language of brief hints
weighted with implications that he need
not elucidate, so that, by the interlocking of
imagery, the work of argument itself is
done by the images. In neither of these

quite different uses of imagery and musical
units is there any suggestion of faltering
power or purpose:

Yet in the trial much opinion dwells.
For here the Trojans taste our dear'st repute
With their fin'st palate. And trust to me, *Ulys-
ses,*
Our imputation shall be oddly pois'd
In this wild action. For the success
(Although particular) shall give a scantling
Of good or bad unto the general.
And in such indexes, although small pricks
To their subsequent volumes, there is seen
The baby figure of the giant mass
Of things to come at large. It is suppos'd
He that meets Hector issues from our choice;
And choice, being mutual act of all our souls,
Makes merit her election, and doth boil,
As 'twere from forth us all, a man distill'd
Out of our virtues; who miscarrying,
What heart receives from hence the conquering
part,
To steel a strong opinion to themselves?
Which entertain'd limbs are his instruments,
In no less working than are swords and bows
Directive by the limbs.

It is this virility, the basis of the style,
running beneath the froth and fantasy of
the Pandarus–Helen scenes, emerging suddenly in a different tempo in Thersites's
ecstasies of abuse, which binds the whole
together, showing one mind at work, and
that an undivided mind, beneath the seeming variations. Moreover, the apposition
(in such a speech as this of Nestor) of
images that, while leading in the reader's
mind to a process equivalent to arguing,
do indeed fly off from each other "with impetuous recoile and jarring sound," plays
its own part in furthering that impression
of disjunction which the art of the play, in
major or in minor form, is ceaselessly at
work to enforce upon us. The persistence,
in fact, of such verse and imagery, right
through to Troilus's last speech on the
death of Hector, indicates, in a very different way but no less surely than the ruthless
choice and the sure handling of material,
that this is no plaything for Shakespeare.
Here is a task upon which his whole mind

was bent in intense and terrific concentration. Metre and imagery alike wrestle with their subject-matter. Every faculty works at its full height; the last resources of intellect and imagination are in action.

The conclusion, then, from even this brief consideration of the subject and form of the play, is that they collaborate, not fortuitously, but intentionally, that the form illuminates and interprets the theme, is itself ordered by it, each being in some degree an aspect of the other, precisely as we expect in a play which is a major work of dramatic art. And so there is confirmed the impression that here is no failure, nor even partial success. For, given discord as the central theme, it is hard to imagine how else it should be formally reflected but in a deliberately intended discord of form also. Rare this may be—perhaps unique in dramatic art—but, as I have suggested, the experience which the play exists to communicate is rare also. As readers, we, in effect, testify, by the conviction that our impression has been conveyed by the whole, and nothing less than the whole play, that the work of art we are contemplating is a living organism, a single form of perceived reality, however vast, complex, or difficult of communication it may be.

With this conviction in mind, then, we can turn to the underlying ideas of the play, no longer expecting to find inconsistency in Shakespeare's treatment of the various parts.

It cannot escape our notice that, in *Troilus and Cressida*, the revelation of the writer's values [4] is not, as in most of Shakespeare's work, implicit only, and so dependent upon our ability to receive the artistic experience of the dramatist [5]; there is also much explicit discussion of the abstract question, "What is value?" This is both easier to distinguish and a direct road to Shakespeare's implicit comment, and for both reasons it is well to consider it first.

Many of the characters—Troilus, Paris, Achilles, Hector, Ulysses, Thersites—are either involved in a bitter fight to harmonize the conflicting evidence of their universe, or are gradually relaxing their efforts and subsiding into a no less bitter equilibrium of disillusionment or loathing. As they make their different interpretations of the meaning or nonmeaning of that universe, it begins to be clear that many of the main issues depend for them upon the question of whether value is absolute or relative; inherent in the object or superimposed upon it; objective or subjective to the valuer.

Troilus, at the beginning of the play, represents one extreme; he believes that the object of faith or worship (a woman, an ideal, a code, an institution) is invested with value precisely to the degree to which it is valued. "What is aught," he exclaims, "but as 'tis valued," and though it never occurs to him to consider the relation of this belief to his estimate of Cressida, there are signs of underlying misgiving in his constant questioning of her. The course of the play brings him out of his belief, through a process of disintegration in which the operation of reasoning is set against the faculty itself,[6] to a state of equilibrium in which he repudiates the two great ideals of his life, love and soldiership, betrayed in the one by Cressida's perfidy, in the other by the murder of Hector. In their romantic defence of the war at the

---

[4] There is some difficulty in finding a term for this. Were the results of Shakespeare's implications positive, the term "values" would be satisfactory. But the modern connotation is, rather, the categories under which a man apprehends the good (see, for example, Inge, *Philosophy of Plotinus*, Vol. II, pp. 74 *seq.*), and, since Shakespeare's conclusion is negative, there is an undesirable element of paradox in applying it here. The position is complicated by the fact that, while his absolutes become evil, he has reached his conclusion by a process of eliminating values. We should perhaps be technically accurate if we said that his metaphysical ultimate is evil manifested in the form of chaos—a negative form perhaps of Nietzsche's "Umwertung aller Werte."

[5] I think that it is still mainly so in *Troilus and Cressida*, and that it is our doubt or inability at this point that has led to the misinterpretation of some of the values indicated in the play.

[6] See *Troilus and Cressida*, V, ii, 139–43.

beginning, he and Paris behave like book collectors who pay £100 for a rare example containing certain typographical peculiarities, not because of its intrinsic beauty or interest, but because that market price has been fixed by other men's willingness to rise to it. For all its romantic dressing, this is at bottom the most purely commercial aspect of value presented in the play, equating merit with the price that can be got for a thing, Helen, with so much warfare. When this is advanced in its turn as a reason for continuing to value her, it involves a bland *petitio principii* that neither of the hot-headed young men has time to observe:

> *Paris.* There's not the meanest spirit on our party
> Without a heart to dare, or sword to draw,
> When Helen is defended. . . . Then (I say)
> Well may we fight for her, whom we know well
> The world's large spaces cannot parallel.

If the fallacy of their arguments escapes their own notice, it does not escape that of Hector, the clearest exponent of the other view of value, value as something that must be primarily inherent in the object valued:

> But value dwells not in particular will;
> It holds his estimate and dignity
> As well wherein 'tis precious of itself,
> As in the prizer: 'Tis mad idolatry
> To make the service greater than the God;
> And the will dotes that is inclinable
> To what infectiously itself affects,
> Without some image of th' affected merit.

It is, as he implies later, for lack of this "image of the affected merit" that the arguments of Paris and Troilus are "glozed but superficially" and are indeed no reasons. He dismisses the strongest argument on their side, namely that its effect on its worshipper itself invests the idol with value (indeed, with all the value we need to seek), temperately making it clear that the sense of value depends for its stability upon something outside itself, objective and absolute, inherent in the object—in short, upon the "image of the affected merit."

But many other characters in the play are seeking, by different methods, and with different incidental experience, for just such an "image"—an absolute value by which to test the evidence of their experience. And they all either come to the same destructive conclusion or themselves furnish notable confirmation by their fates of the destructive philosophies of the rest.

Achilles, lazy in mind and body, is, when roused, no more defective in intelligence than he is in professional skill. The sting of Agamemnon's insults drives him to some effortless and quite lucid self-examination on the nature of reputation and, as he falls in with Ulysses at the peak of his exasperation, the discussion slides naturally into the major question of the play, "Is there or is there not in anything an absolute value?" Achilles makes for himself the discovery that reputation (which he, being of the school of Troilus and Paris, equates with value) determines a man's own view of himself. Ulysses clinches it for him: a man "feels not what he owes [= owns], but by reflection," but he carries the investigation a step further, and sees in reputation (the value other men put upon a man) the necessary completion of a process without which a quality does not fully exist. He equates it with the function of communication as we understand it in art or in love, without some form of which the process has not been consummated. Indeed, Shakespeare lets him use that very term:

> No man is the lord of any thing,
> (Though in and of him there is much consisting)
> Till he communicate his parts to others:
> Nor doth he of himself know them for ought,
> Till he behold them formed in th' applause,
> Where they are extended.

The essential relation between "communication" and "form" here is highly significant, as is the distinction between Ulysses' position and that of Troilus, Paris, and Achilles. Ulysses, who could speak later of the "mystery, wherein relation Durst never meddle, in the soul of state," does not deny the possibility of the absolute value that Hector insists on. He merely points out the inseparable relationship between the two aspects, intrinsic value and assessed value, in man's experience, and declares that without the second the first is unfulfilled. "Else a great prince in prison lies."

When we remember how unusual are discussions of abstract themes in Shakespeare's plays as compared, for instance, with Chapman's, Tourneur's, and Beaumont and Fletcher's among his contemporaries, we may well pause to ask what it means in *Troilus and Cressida*. In all the plays in which something similar occurs (and never, not even in *Measure for Measure*, is it so full and so penetrating) it is also strictly integral to the main matter and so inwoven with the action as to be a natural commentary upon it. This is no less true of the discussions on the nature of kingship and government in the sequence of history plays, especially the two parts of *Henry IV* and *Henry V*, than of the reflections on the art of conduct in *Hamlet*. Arguing from this, we may wonder whether this continual talk of values, this debating to and fro not only of their nature, but of the question of their existence, is not equally essential in some way to the fundamental theme of *Troilus and Cressida*, whether, in short, Shakespeare ever suffered his characters to be deeply concerned with a question which was not the core of the play. Is Shakespeare, in *Troilus and Cressida*, himself revealing, through their conscious analyses as through their experience, a state in which such questions met just such answers in his own mind? I think he is, and I think this brings us to the root of the matter. The writer of this play is a man to whom values have become suspect.

Were the wisdom of Hector and Ulysses allowed to survive, in contrast with the rest of the play but without further comment, this might be less clearly implied. But actually it suffers defeat in both cases; in Hector's by the implications of his betrayal at the hands of a code in whose stability he

had trusted; in Ulysses', first by the course of the action, which denies the truth of his idea by the contradiction of event, and, secondly and more specifically, by a later admission of his own, when, arguing that virtue must not seek "remuneration for the thing it is," he goes on to dismiss the possibility of intrinsic value having, in practice and in the affairs of men, any effective alliance with assessed value:

> Love, friendship, charity, are subjects all
> To envious and calumniating time:

so that the indispensable condition, without which intrinsic value cannot be liberated into reality, is never there. The reason for this is at once simple and irremediable, it lies in the nature of man's mind:

> One touch of nature makes the whole world kin:
> That all with one consent praise new born gauds,
> Though they are made and moulded of things past,
> And give to dust, that is a little gilt,
> More laud than gilt o'er-dusted.

That is, man's judgement (his capacity for valuing) is incapable of its task, and absolute value, whether or not it exists, is never discernible.

Even the acute intelligence of Ulysses then, having done its best upon the problem, has met with implicit and explicit defeat, and it is not surprising that the same fate befalls the other characters.

The last position, in descending order of negation, is that of Thersites. He has long taken for granted the conclusion that Ulysses has implied; mankind in his eyes is as incapable of worthy judgement as of worthy conduct; Ulysses, Nestor, Agamemnon, Hector, and Troilus are reduced to their lowest terms, no less than Achilles, Ajax, Patroclus, Paris, Helen, and Cressida. But he has travelled further. He does not waste time debating the existence of absolute value, or whether or not man can perceive and live by it; he assumes no criterion beyond that fallible human judgement of which he is so eloquent a satirist. Nor does the obscene casualty of fate and circumstance stagger him; for here the paradoxes of circumstances have long ago taken the wind of satire: "To what form but that he is, should wit larded with malice, and malice forced with wit turn him to? To an ass were nothing; he is both ass and ox; to an ox, were nothing; he is both ox and ass." In the world he offers us there is no stability in character, ideals, institutions, judgement, nor in imagination itself. The whole is a shifting, heaving morass where all is relative and nothing absolute, where pullulating worm and insect forms, seething upon the surface, are seen suddenly, as at the dissipating of some soft, concealing cloud, intent upon their task of disintegration and erosion, reducing all things to their own terms and substance.

And yet Thersites is an integral part of the play's form and matter, and that play is a living organism. It is upon the whole fabric that his mind is at work, driven by the passion of his disgust to break down the forms of things into lifeless elements that can never again be human flesh and blood nor even wholesome earth, but must remain barren and negative like deflowered soil. As we read his comment and relate it with the debates in these other minds, his is seen to be the dominant of their scale. For he, to whom all the argument is a cuckold and a whore, who sees the common curse of mankind, folly and ignorance, as deserving only the dry serpigo and war and lechery to confound them, has arrived at his conclusion by the very road that they are travelling—Ulysses by his own reasoning, Troilus by the conversion wrought in him by event, and the rest by their betrayal of or at the hands of their codes. The starting-point of his interpretation is the conclusion to which they too are proceeding: there is no absolute value inherent in the universe imaged in the loves and wars of Greeks and Trojans. There *is* no "image of the affected merit."

Once we have isolated this central ques-

tion (What is the nature of value and has it or has it not an absolute existence?), once we have traced the series of positions, from positive to negative, of Hector, Troilus, Ulysses, and Thersites and the relation of each of those positions to the general evidence of the play, matter and form alike are seen to derive from this conclusion, which makes of the whole a vast, complex but organic artistic experience. The conflict between conduct, ideals, and event which the choice of material lays so clearly before us and the idea of disjunction inescapably enforced by the structure of the play serve now to drive home the conclusion that in this play disjunction was a fundamental principle, if not the most fundamental, in Shakespeare's view of the universe of event.

But we are uneasily aware, at the same time, that this judgement is not limited to the universe of event. Were that so, we should probably find in this play a mood of partial negation only, as in the balanced conflicts of the tragedies, where the positive element contends on equal terms with the negative and the duality is essential in the artistic experience. But in *Troilus and Cressida* our sense of the artistic unity has derived, as we have realized, not from an impression of balance, but from an impression of evil enveloping apparent good; not from a picture of the accidental prevalence of mischance and injustice over wisdom and rectitude, but from the implication of a causal relation between disjunction in event and the absence of absolute criteria in the universe of thought. To make this clear we may look again at some of the noblest thought in the play and see how it is related to the enveloping and prevailing evil and how its destruction carries the principle of disjunction into the domain of the mind itself.

Let us take again Ulysses' defence of "degree," the foundation upon which civilization and its achievement rests. The hierarchy of his state stands, in its nobility of conception, linked with the hierarchy of the heavens, a microcosm of the great universe:

> The Heavens themselves, the planets, and this centre,
> Observe degree, priority, and place,

and "all in line of order." The heavens maintain their courses and the world of man reflects their ordered process in "The unity and married calm of states." But if the planets "in evil mixture to disorder wander," then "Degree is shak'd," both in the cosmos and in society, the image of the cosmos created by man's mind. Then, in the two universes alike, in that of the material cosmos and that of man's creating, "each thing meets in mere oppugnancy," and chaos is come again. To this "mere oppugnancy" the play leads us inescapably, by the matter and texture of the concluding acts. The towering thoughts and ideals topple down before a destiny as implacable as that foreseen by Ulysses for the doomed towers of Troy; and if we look immediately from these ideals to the last phases of the action, the ambush and murder of Hector, we have no choice but to measure the chaos and the discord by the gracious assurance, the magnanimity, and the seeming stability that they destroy. Just as we feel the value of the *Oedipus* or the *Oresteia* to be in one way commensurate with the depth and the power of evil which Sophocles and Aeschylus meet and transmute, so in *Troilus* the nobility of that order which in the end proves perishable gives us the measure of the destructive forces which triumph over it. The existence of the principle of cause and order (in the cosmos and in the affairs of men) is therein questioned; it vanishes, revealing destruction as the principle underlying all life.

The supreme reach, moreover, of Shakespeare's imagery and prosody in this play, with all that they imply of sustained imaginative thought, serve also by their association with the prevailing evil, to affirm the magnitude and universality of that evil when it does prevail:

> But the strong base and building of my love
> Is as the very centre of the earth,
> Drawing all things to it.

It is Cressida speaking; and when the base of the world, the centre of stability itself, is equated with Cressida's love, we have not much farther to seek for Shakespeare's comment upon that stability.

Moreover, the downfall of the principles of order and value in the world of man's creation, with the substitution of the negative principles of disjunction and chaos, is traced directly to that inability in man to imagine absolute value which we have already recognized; in Ulysses's words, to the "touch of nature" that "makes the whole world kin." It *is*, indeed, man's "nature." Not only is the objective universe, then, the cosmos and society, found subject to this curse of disjunction; the universe of the imagination also is proved incapable of conceiving a stable value. Disjunction, chaos, discord in the spheres, this is the only irreducible and continuing thing. The denial of absolute value, of any real "image of the affected merit," is, then, carried beyond the world of event within the play; casualty has replaced causality in the world of the imagination also.

It would seem, then, that this play is an attempt, upon a scale whose vastness is measured by the intensity with which every faculty of the poet's mind is engaged, to find that image (of absolute value) in the evidence of man's achievement, in the sum or parts of his experience or, if nowhere else, in the processes of creative imagination. Troilus's love, Agamemnon's chivalry, Ulysses's vision of the hierarchy of state are all, thus, experimental images, in which are tested the absolute value of man's passion, intellect, and imagination. In face of this test, this "Quid hoc ad aeternitatem?", all fail. There is no absolute quality the evidence for which does not resolve itself into a mere subjective illusion of blood or fancy, a

> mad idolatry,
> To make the service greater than the God.

The creations of man's spirit, hitherto exalted, are now seen to have survived only by chance, at the mercy all the time of a stronger, natural law of destruction; what in another mood might have appeared tragic accidents, the counterpoint in a fuller harmony, are now seen, instead, to reveal an underlying law to which all is recurrently and inescapably subject. This is the ultimate, indeed the only surviving absolute in *Troilus and Cressida*. The faculty that could perceive degree and the ordered form of a universe, the imagination itself, has been touched and the images of form no longer rise at its command. "There is no more to say." The dark night of the soul comes down upon the unilluminated wreckage of the universe of vision. The play of *Troilus and Cressida* remains as one of the few living and unified expressions of this experience.

The grand scale of this catastrophe blinds us. We do not willingly imagine this overthrow; some at least of us never to the end comprehend it, for it is like a note too deep for our hearing, or a landscape too vast for our experiencing. We probably come nearer to understanding the tragedies than this play which is no tragedy and is yet perhaps the record of the profoundest catastrophe in man's experience.

> Moving of th' earth brings harms and fears,
>   Men reckon what it did and meant,
> But trepidation of the spheres,
>   Though greater far, is innocent.

If we turn from this attempt to understand the nature of the underlying ideas in *Troilus and Cressida* and consider the form through which these ideas are revealed, we see that what has been achieved is in fact what we suggested at the outset. The idea of chaos, of disjunction, of ultimate formlessness and negation, has by a supreme act of artistic mastery been given form. It has not been described in more or less abstract terms; it has been imaged. What seemed to be an absolute limitation of drama has been

transcended and shown, in this rare achievement, to be but relative.

And in this case, even more than in either of those which we have just considered, the subduing of content to form is no mere act of virtuosity; it has a further significance as an instance of one of the ultimate functions of art.

That the experience on which this play rests is of profound significance at any time, and of peculiar significance to our own, needs no discussion. Whenever actual experience threatens to pass endurance, there is a measure of alleviation in discovering that it has already been met and recorded. The facts are not softened, but the sense of isolation which gives the facts a main part of their horror is mitigated; the desert is no less to be reckoned with, but something is gone if it is no longer "terra incognita" nor utterly unmapped. When we find, as we certainly do in this play, not merely a record of actual experience, but a communication of an artistic experience, the alleviation becomes more positive; the actual experience, in that case, has not only been met, but resolved into form by the grandest of all human faculties, the artistic imagination. Once it has been encompassed by this imagination, at whatever cost, the bounds of human comprehension have been set forward in proportion as it had appeared incomprehensible. The value that we finally attach, in this way, to Aeschylus, to Sophocles, and to Shakespeare rests upon the extent of their comprehension of evil, and upon the extent to which that vision of evil has been brought under the governance of those artistic laws which are themselves the image of the ultimate law of an ordered universe. Thus, in Shakespeare's *Troilus and Cressida* we meet a paradoxical dualism. The content of his thought is an implacable assertion of chaos as the ultimate fact of being; the presence of artistic form is a deeper, unconscious testimony to an order which is actually ultimate and against which the gates of hell shall not prevail.

This is made clearer still by the direction his thought takes in the plays that follow *Troilus and Cressida* and lead on in direct succession to the final group. This subduing of matter to form in the earlier play is then seen to be prophetic of a resolution not only of the technical problem of relating content to form, but of the dualism of thought implied in their conflict. The victory of form is no mere technical achievement; it has, as has form in all great art, a spiritual aspect and significance.

It is the development from *Troilus and Cressida* to the latest group of plays that gives to both their profoundest meaning. Our understanding of the latest plays bears strict equivalence with our understanding of this one; only so far as we imagine the abomination of desolation can we imagine beatitude. For the tragedies that follow represent a recovery of the balance between the perception of evil and a positive interpretation of it, whereas in *Troilus and Cressida* the writer looks upon the implacable fact of orderless evil in the mind and in the objective universe alike. In this play the judgement is unshaken, and there is no escape from the torment of the perception of evil, but in the later plays judgement is superseded. The conclusions from all its experiments meet in the tense yet motionless equilibrium of Troilus's last speech, but the revelations perceived by the mode of thought that supersedes it flash out in sudden phrases on the lips of Edgar, Gloucester, and Lear:

> Sit gods upon your thrones, and smile at Troy.
> I say at once, let your brief plagues be mercy,
> And linger not our sure destructions on. . . .
> I do not speak of flight, of fear, of death,
> But dare all imminence that gods and men,
> Address their dangers in. . . . But march away:
> Hector is dead: there is no more to say.

"Let your brief plagues be mercy"; Edgar in *Lear* learns at length that "the worst is not, So long as we can say this is the worst," and his discovery rests upon the knowledge, carried over from *Troilus and*

Cressida, that when we are at the worst "there is no more to say."

In the next phase of this experience, then, there is no longer this vigilant judgement presiding over implacable fact, for a breakup has set in and disintegration has overpowered judgement. In the picture offered by *Timon,* the play which appears to reveal the next phase in this progression, the universe of thought and imagination is riven almost beyond recognition and the matter and form of the play derive from the experience, not of imminent disjunction, but of chaos itself. This brings its own anaesthesia and, though the powers of the mind seem to have surrendered to disintegration, something that was invisible at the stage of *Troilus and Cressida* is beginning to appear. The "strong base of the world" has indeed now broken up, but through the rift is revealed, at depths almost below man's vision, a new base not dreamed of, where the "perpetual-sober gods" remain, untouched even by the "trepidation of the spheres." The emergence from destructive to constructive experience has begun again, though it may be revealed in *Timon* only in this one phrase. Our experience of each play is, I venture to think, incomplete without the other.

In *Lear* the indications of this are more frequent and the conversions that flow in rising and cumulative waves through the last two acts of the play all set towards a positive, though undefined, interpretation, resting upon this foundation. The tragic balance is readjusted. The perception of evil is as full as in the *Oedipus* or the *Oresteia,* but there is an undefined, but no less positive, perception of order emerging again from casualty.

> *Glouc.* O you mighty Gods!
> This world I do renounce, and, in your sights,
> Shake patiently my great affliction off;
> If I could bear it longer, and not fall
> To quarrel with your great opposeless wills,
> My snuff and loathed part of nature should
> Burn itself out.

· · · · · ·

You ever gentle Gods, take my breath from me,
Let not my worser spirit tempt me again
To die before you please.
                  . . . What are you?
     Edgar. A most poor man, made tame to for-
         tune's blows
Who, by the art of known and feeling sorrows,
Am pregnant to good pity.

There is, of course, no actual refutation of the conclusions of *Troilus*. The commentary of *Lear* is rather a series of flashes out into a seemingly limitless universe of positive ideas and later plays extend and stabilize these. But this kind of commentary does, by its very non-logical process, indicate in part how the universe of *Troilus* was superseded. The brief visions of circumambient reality, the "perpetual-sober Gods," the "great opposeless wills," the "ever-gentle Gods," suggest that the imagination may in this way perceive what, in the earlier play, operating in a field of actuality delimited by the judgement, it could not; Edgar could, if he chose, refute Ulysses's argument, that intrinsic value can never become effective because man's judgement is preoccupied with assessed value, by pointing out that it contains an undistributed middle on the grand scale.

Simultaneously there comes into sight that earlier mood again in which,

There's not the smallest orb which thou beholdest
But in his motion like an angel sings,
Still quiring to the young-eyed cherubins;
Such harmony is in immortal souls.

and that, slightly later, in which Pericles, in face of the opening vision of a universe of fundamental order and reconciliation, finds again the image in which Shakespeare has clothed this idea, whether negative or positive, throughout:

Per.   . . . But what music?
Hel. My Lord I hear none.
Per. None? The music of the spheres.

Already we are in sight of the harmony of the latest plays, and the seeming finality of the vision of *Troilus and Cressida* is seen to be, after all, not an end, but the birth of a new, infinitely extended and positive vision. At the phase at which Lear completes and resolves the experience of Troilus and Cressida, only the anticipation of this is indicated. *Plus ultra.* "It is enough that there *is* a beyond."

Robert Ornstein

Troilus and Cressida

AFTER the melancholy deeps of *Hamlet*, *Troilus and Cressida* and *Measure for Measure* seem strange interludes of mockery and denigration, retreats from the tragedy of evil to the comedy of vice. They are problems if not problem plays, "un-Shakespearean" in temper and viewpoint, ambiguous in characterization. They seem to turn ideals of chivalry, justice, and mercy seamy side out. The lecher leers over the virgin's shoulder; the romantic idealist falls in love with a whore; one touch of nature in the loins makes the whole world kin. But they are not so much comical satires as dialectical dramas in the manner of *Byron's Conspiracy*; like Chapman's play they approach the issues of tragedy ironically and analytically, and thus engage the intellect more than the imagination. If by comparison to the *Iliad* and the medieval gestes of Troy, *Troilus* seems a mockery of heroism, it is not contemptuous of the virtues which men sacrifice at the altar of war. Behind the joke of Achilles' cowardice and Pandarus' aching bones lies a serious study of man's aspiration toward the ideal in love and war.

In *Troilus* Shakespeare explores the paradoxical truth that war and lechery—the most primitive human activities—have from the dawn of civilization excited man's highest poetic faculties. The heroic legend immortalizes the conflicting dualities of man's nature and poses the central problem of his quest for ideal values. Chained to the earth by animal desires, condemned by mortality to the tyranny of time, man nevertheless hungers for a dedication that will give permanent significance to his life. Even in the savagery of war he learns some final truth about his humanity; even in untimely death he satisfies a hunger for experience that might otherwise be unfilled. Religion and philosophy escape the oppression of time by postulating eternal metaphysical values. The chivalric ideal challenges time with an appropriate recklessness by exalting the transitory qualities of youth, beauty, and strength and by placing its absolutes within the realm of mortality. By sophisticating primitive impulses with ceremonial ritual, it heightens and glorifies the sensation of life that flames in the brief orgiastic pleasure of love and war. It finds its eternity in the ecstatic moments of sexual possession and military conquest, the ancient complementary proofs of manhood and virility.

The Homeric myth tells of a decade of slaughter for the possession of a beautiful woman; the analytic intellect seeks a more realistic and complex motive for human sacrifice. It cannot believe that men died for the sake of a faithless woman, especially after years of futile, senseless struggle. Logic insists that ultimately both sides must have despised Helen. And thus Diomedes speaks for the Greeks:

> She's bitter to her country. Hear me, Paris:
> For every false drop in her bawdy veins
> A Grecian's life hath sunk; for every scruple
> Of her contaminated carrion weight
> A Troyan hath been slain. Since she could speak,
> She hath not given so many good words breath
> As for her Greeks and Troyans suff'red death.
> (IV. i. 68–74)

Reprinted with permission of the copyright owners, the Regents of the University of Wisconsin, from *The Moral Vision of Jacobean Tragedy* (Madison: University of Wisconsin Press, 1960), pp. 240–49.

Hector expresses the same thought with greater courtesy when he pleads:

> Let Helen go.
> Since the first sword was drawn about this question,
> Every tithe soul 'mongst many thousand dismes
> Hath been as dear as Helen. I mean, of ours.
> If we have lost so many tenths of ours
> To guard a thing not ours nor worth to us
> (Had it our name) the value of one ten,
> What merit's in that reason which denies
> The yielding of her up?   (II. ii. 17–25)

Here is the wearisome condition of warring mankind: two great civilizations locked in mortal combat for the sake of a woman whom neither side desires, corrupted and enervated by seven years of futile struggle but still unwilling to sacrifice the principle of honor for which the war is being fought.

The conflict between Trojan and Greek has many analogues in Shakespeare's drama. It is foreshadowed by the opposition between Richard and Bolingbroke and Hotspur and Hal, and it is recalled by the dichotomy of Egypt and Rome in *Antony and Cleopatra*. On one side is a decaying world of chivalry, courtly and romantic, softened by feminine influence and refined in sensibility. On the other side is a purely masculine, realistic world of soldiery and empire, pragmatic in its values, uncritical of its goals, concerned only with the attainment of power. The character of Troilus expresses the doomed, tainted nobility of a highly sophisticated yet immature civilization. He unites the impetuous valor of Hotspur and the romantic ardor of the inexperienced Romeo; he is the hero of medieval saga and the lover of the Renaissance sonnet cycles. His restless spirit protests the dullness of life; he shares Hotspur's contempt for wariness and for niggling calculations of profit and loss— for the *quid pro quo* by which reason determines the value of things. Like Chapman's early heroes, he would subjugate the material world to his poetic imagination. He speaks for the individual will against the restrictions and decorums of society.

The result of Troilus' romanticism is philosophical anarchy, but his ideal of honor is consistent in its premises. He has no illusions about the value of Helen. On the contrary, he exults in her soilure because it bears witness to the ideality of Troy's chivalric adventure. If the possession of a faithless drab were the goal of battle, then the cause would be worthless; but Helen is merely a symbol of the real issue. The Greeks do not want her; they seek to impose their will on Troy, and honor demands that the chivalric will be free and unconquered. Moreover the real enemy is not the Greek soldier but stagnation, the rusting of unused strength and vitality. Even if Helen is not worth the spilling of a single drop of blood, she is nevertheless

> a theme of honour and renown,
> A spur to valiant and magnanimous deeds,
> Whose present courage may beat down our foes,
> And fame in time to come canonize us.
>   (II. ii. 199–202)

To the romantic ego, man is the measurer of all things; nothing has value except as he treasures it. Against the realist's credo that the value of an object is its selling price (what other men will pay for it), Troilus sets forth the romantic ideal that the only significant values are those intangibles which a man will not sell at the price of his own life.

Hector protests the complete subjectivity of Troilus' idealism. He pleads for objective criteria of judgment, for a recognition of the absolute, "natural" values which reason determines and which inhere in the customs of society. Whereas Troilus sweeps aside moral considerations as irrelevant, Hector argues the immorality of keeping Helen:

> Nature craves
> All dues be rend'red to their owners. Now
> What nearer debt in all humanity
> Than wife is to the husband? If this law
> Of nature be corrupted through affection,
> And that great minds, of partial indulgence
> To their benumbed wills, resist the same,

There is a law in each well-ord'red nation
To curb those raging appetites that are
Most disobedient and refractory.
If Helen then be wife to Sparta's king
(As it is known she is), these moral laws
Of nature and of nations speak aloud
To have her back return'd. Thus to persist
In doing wrong extenuates not wrong,
But makes it much more heavy.

(II. ii. 173–88)

Here is the voice of sanity and reason but not necessarily of objective judgment. If value does not dwell in the "particular will," then it does not dwell either in general opinion. The mere accumulation of subjective judgments does not, as Montaigne noted, create objective values, nor does the stamp of custom approve what is "natural." Once the question of values is raised, it is legitimate to ask, "What is reason but as 'tis valu'd?" Actually Hector is more of a romanticist than Troilus; he would be the Red Cross Knight, the chivalric defender of rational ideals. Troilus sees more realistically that honor and reason lead in opposite directions:

Nay, if we talk of reason,
Let's shut our gates and sleep. Manhood and
honour
Should have hare hearts, would they but fat
their thoughts
With this cramm'd reason. Reason and respect
Make livers pale and lustihood deject.

(II. ii. 46–50)

If it is "mad idolatry/To make the service greater than the god," it is the only idolatry appropriate to the god of war. For how many military causes were worth the waste and misery which they entailed? There is rarely a "reason" for war except for the loathsome truth which honor hides, that men want to fight.

It is a measure of Troy's corruption that the *débat* between Hector and Troilus is purely theoretical, a courtly charade that ends with Hector's announcement that he has sent his personal challenge to the Greeks. The Trojan heroes not only hold their honors dearer than their lives but dearer also than the lives of thousands of defenseless countrymen. Because there is no "cause" for battle, their dedication to honor is in fact a dedication to personal vanity. And yet there is a terrible innocence in Troilus' self-deception. By making theoretical abstractions out of his egoistic desires, he assumes that he has elevated them above the materialism of life and turned the "performance of his heaving spleen" into a metaphysical value. He is scornful of ordinary getting and spending but he chaffers for honor on the battlefield by selling other men's lives. Exalting the individual judgment over vulgar opinion, he nevertheless takes as his absolute the "immortal" reputation that rests on the giddy props of other men's memories. By refusing to calculate the cost of the war because honor is at stake, he discards as worthless the very Trojan lives his valor protects. Actually he is not an intellectual anarchist because he recognizes as valid only his own subjective conclusions.

Troilus is Shakespeare's most subtle study of narcissistic infatuation. The defense of a slut and the worship of a wanton suffice as mirrors to reflect his image as a chivalric lover. He is not gulled by Cressida's pose of modesty, nor is she a hypocrite. She is a daughter of the game which men would have her play and for which they despise her. She sees beneath the ceremonies of courtly love the commerce of desire in which all selling prices are artificial and the pleasure of possession unequal to the thrill of anticipation. More realist than sensualist, more wary and weary than wanton, she is alone in Troy and defenseless among the Greeks. Like Troilus she believes that women are as they are valued, but she is too experienced to place a value on her affections that is different from her worth in men's eyes. To Troilus she is the Lesbia of the sonnets, but the rest of Troy assesses her at a lower rate. And she sees from her treatment by Diomedes and the other Greeks that her price has fallen still further. Having lost

Troilus except for the nightly "visitations" which will satisfy his appetite, she sells when she can—she is not for all markets.

To view Cressida's infidelity as a cynical traducement of the ideal of courtly love is to miss the larger commentary which Shakespeare makes upon the masculine ego. The brutal casualness with which Diomedes "wins" his lady satisfies more frankly and grossly the same impulse that lies behind Troilus' romanticism. The worshipping of a courtly mistress and the moaning anguish of an unrequited lover are poses that enhance the value of sexual possession. They afford an opportunity for self-dramatization; they enable the "refined" sensibility to prolong by anticipation the transient ecstasy of sexual union. What are women but as they are valued *by men?* Troy would not sell Helen, its theme of honor, for the price of survival, but it barters Cressida for a single prisoner. The noble Hector uses Andromache's beauty and chastity as the subject of his martial brag but when she begs him to avoid the fatal battle, he rudely thrusts her away and orders her into the palace. When his honor is at pawn, he owes a higher obligation to his enemy than to his wife.

Even as Troilus intellectualizes the chivalric code of Troy, Ulysses exemplifies the pragmatic realism of the Greeks. Astute, ruthless, cunning, he is Shakespeare's ultimate characterization of the politician, whose art is the manipulation of other men's ambitions and desires. Like the Trojans, the Greek leaders hold a council of state, but they are not concerned with the value of the war, only with a strategy that will bring it to a swift and successful conclusion. Seven years of futile bloodletting have eroded the Grecian spirit. Dissension, envy, and discontent have destroyed martial discipline and sapped the will to victory. Achilles lies in his tent, enamored of a Trojan woman, jeering at his leaders. The pompous Agamemnon lacks the qualities of leadership, and Menelaus, the cuckold, is universally despised. Although superior in force of arms, the Greek army is impotent and incapable of storming the gates of Troy.

Ulysses assesses the situation shrewdly. This is no time to probe the ulcer of a worthless cause. The demoralized Greeks must be distracted from the sordid circumstances of the war by a contemplation of metaphysical harmonies; the illusion of common counsel must be obtained by reference to abstract assumptions on which all men agree. Although Ulysses requires no soaring lecture on order and degree to diagnose the disease which rots the Grecian spirit, we detect no trace of irony or hypocrisy in his magnificent and oft-quoted speech. After all, this is the kind of abstract idealism which does not commit the realist to any particular course or code of action, and which comfortably reaffirms Ulysses' position in the Greek hierarchy against Thersites' cynicism and Achilles' rebellious pride. Because his idealism lies outside the realm of political action, he can at one time describe the universal order of nature and at another time remind Achilles that one touch of nature makes the whole world kin in frailty and giddiness. He can speak of the correspondence between the microcosm of the state and the macrocosm of the universe and then remark that honor, degree, and high estate in the little world of man rest upon ephemeral opinion.

We expect from the experienced and clear-sighted Ulysses a truly objective assessment of value. We find, however, that Ulysses has no opinions of his own on the worth of glory, honor, war, and love. He is an expert critic of other men's opinions; his most penetrating observations are on the vagaries of mob psychology:

> Let not virtue seek
> Remuneration for the thing it was!
> For beauty, wit,
> High birth, vigour of bone, desert in service,
> Love, friendship, charity, are subjects all
> To envious and calumniating Time.
> One touch of nature makes the whole world kin,

That all with one consent praise new-born
    gauds,
Though they are made and moulded of things
    past,
And give to dust that is a little gilt
More laud than gilt o'erdusted.
                      (III. iii. 169–79)

Without illusion, the realist is a connois-
seur of other men's illusions; indeed, their
illusions are the only realities with which
he is actively concerned, the only ones on
which he bases his calculations. If there
are permanent and intrinsic values, they
do not enter into or influence the course
of political maneuver. Trapped in the same
circumstances that corrupt Achilles and
Troilus, Ulysses maintains his intellectual
clarity by withholding all judgment except
on the practical issues of war and state.
Thus in a way his poised rational objectiv-
ity is more subversive of values than Troilus' impetuous romanticism. He is the
Shakespearean analogue of Warwick in *St.
Joan:* the urbane, civilized statesman, free
from dangerous enthusiasms or prejudices,
who is capable of instigating atrocities
because he recognizes only political necessities.

Ulysses' policy brings Troy to its ap-
pointed doom. As in the "Henriad" and in
Antony and Cleopatra, the realist defeats
the romanticist, the politician vanquishes
the chevalier, the masculine world of ambition and empire subjugates the more
feminine world of courtly ceremony. In
Troilus, however, the pattern of events
seems too overtly dialectical; intellectual
analysis robs the heroic fable of its inherent pathos. The waste of beauty, youth, and
valor does not achieve personal and poignant significance in the fates of Hector
and Troilus because they exist as characters only to exemplify a thesis. They are
actors in an intellectual drama whose
meaning they never comprehend; they are
doomed by circumstances and by the
tainted values of the civilization which they
lead to destruction. Because the burden of
redeeming a worthless cause rests on their

shoulders, they grow more and more infatuated with honor, until the pursuit of a
"goodly armour" leads Hector into the
cowardly ambush by which Achilles re-
gains his "reputation." The Greeks are
equally driven by "necessity." Although
Ulysses correctly diagnoses the disease of
pride and emulation that infects Agamemnon's army, he dares not cure the disease
because there is no other incentive to heroic action than the thirst for reputation.
Universal law may demand that pride be
checked, but political necessity demands
that arrogance, envy, and stupidity be in-
tensified and exploited. Sold like merchan-
dise, the bartered Cressida becomes a Grecian drab because the difference between a
courtly mistress and a common stale lies
not in what men desire of her but how they
treat her. The most exquisite courtesan of
the *ancien régime* would have become the
local trollop in an obscure army camp; for
while an aristocratic courtier will pay with
words, vows, and deeds for the faith of his
mistress, the less refined soldier will pay
a smaller price for a more temporary gratification.

Troilus' romantic ideal demands that
Cressida be faithful; his self-esteem demands that she be true to *him.* As he
watches her submit too easily and coyly to
Diomedes, his ego is more deeply wounded
than his heart; he suffers without illumination:

This she? No, this is Diomed's Cressida!
If beauty have a soul, this is not she;
If souls guide vows, if vows be sanctimonies
If sanctimony be the gods' delight,
If there be rule in unity itself—
This is not she. O madness of discourse,
That cause sets up with and against itself!
Bifold authority! where reason can revolt
Without perdition, and loss assume all reason
Without revolt: this is, and is not, Cressid!
Within my soul there doth conduce a fight
Of this strange nature, that a thing inseparate
Divides more wider than the sky and earth;
And yet the spacious breadth of this division
Admits no orifex for a point as subtle
As Ariachne's broken woof to enter.

Instance, O instance! strong as Pluto's gates:
Cressid is mine, tied with the bonds of heaven.
Instance, O instance! strong as heaven itself:
The bonds of heaven are slipp'd, dissolv'd, and
loos'd.   (V. ii. 137–56)

Troilus is not disillusioned; he projects his inner confusion into a law of universal chaos and would have us believe that because *his* vanity is stricken the bonds of heaven are slipped. If he were a more consistent philosopher, he would realize that he has no reason to complain, for if the individual mind sets the value of all things, then Diomedes is entitled to his estimate of Cressida's worth and she to her estimate of Troilus' affections.

Out of the sordidness of Cressida's infidelity, however, a new romantic cause is born. Another soiled woman becomes the theme of chivalric honor and the cause for senseless struggle. Now Troilus rages after Diomedes; now Diomedes assumes a courtly pose and dedicates Troilus' horse to his whore. The tables turn, the charade of chivalry approaches burlesque, but one touch of nature still makes the world kin. When Hector dies the charade ends: the appetite for glory reverts to a primitive bloodlust, for chivalry is a luxury which only the winner can afford. Refusing to calculate the cost of Hector's death lest it destroy the Trojan will to combat, Troilus has no reason to fight except for the savage impulse to kill. And after he and Ulysses have commented on the frailty of affection, it is only fitting that Pandarus should have his chance to speak. Naturally Pandarus is disappointed with Troilus' ingratitude. Even a bawd has feelings, and though he derived a vicarious pleasure from trading in flesh, his negotiations for Troilus were more selfless and "innocent" than the heroic idealism that doomed Troy.

The comic complaints of a syphilitic bawd end the play on a note of derision that seems to vindicate Thersites' scabrous cynicism. Yet the total impression of *Troilus* is hardly nihilistic. It is a depressing play, not because it establishes the futility of man's search for ideal values but because it is a sociological and psychological analysis of decadent values. Like Ulysses, Shakespeare is concerned here only with the nature of man's illusions, not with the essential worth of his ideals. The gestes of Troy do not mock the selfless dedication of Cordelia and Kent; however, they provide an ironic gloss for the chivalric gesture that costs Edmund his victory and his life.

Edward Dowden

The Role of Helena

IN *All's Well that Ends Well*, a subject of extreme difficulty, when regarded on the ethical side, was treated by Shakspere with a full consciousness of its difficulty. A woman who seeks her husband, and gains him against his will; who afterwards by a fraud—a fraud however pious—defeats his intention of estranging her, and becomes the mother of his child; such a personage it would seem a sufficiently difficult task to render attractive or admirable. Yet Helena has been named by Coleridge "the loveliest of Shakspere's characters." Possibly Coleridge recognized in Helena the single quality which, if brought to bear upon himself by one to whom he yielded love and worship, would have given definiteness and energy to his somewhat vague and incoherent life. For sake of this one thing Shakspere was interested in the story, and so admirable did it seem to him that he could not choose but endeavor to make beautiful and noble the entire character and action of Helena. This one thing is the energy, the leap up, the direct advance of the *will* of Helena, her prompt, unerroneous tendency towards the right and efficient *deed*. She does not display herself through her words; she does not, except on rarest occasions, allow her feelings to expand and deploy themselves; her entire force of character is concentrated in what she does. And therefore we see her quite as much indirectly, through the effect which she has produced upon other persons of the drama, as through self-confession or immediate presentation of her character.

A motto for the play may be found in the words uttered with pious astonishment by the clown, when his mistress bids him to begone, "That man should be at woman's command, and yet no hurt done." Helena is the providence of the play; and there is "no hurt done," but rather healing—healing of the body of the French king, healing of the spirit of the man she loves. For Bertram, when the story begins, though endowed with beauty and bravery and the advantages (and disadvantages) of rank, is in character, in heart, in will, a crude, ungracious boy. Helena loves him, and sets him, in her love, above herself, the poor physician's daughter, out of her sphere:

> 'Twere all one
> That I should love a bright, particular star
> And think to wed it, he is so above me.

She loves him thus, but (if love can be conceived as distinct from liking) she does not wholly like him. She admits to herself that in worship of Bertram there is a certain fatuousness—

> Now he's gone, and my idolatrous fancy
> Must sanctify his reliques.

She sees from the first that the friend of his choice, the French captain, is "a notorious liar," "solely a coward," "a great way fool"; she trembles for what Bertram may learn at the court.

> God send him well!
> The court's a learning place; and he is one—
> *Parol.* What one i' faith?
> *Hel.* That I wish well.

Yet she sees in Bertram a potential nobleness waiting to be evoked. And her will leaps forward to help him. Now she loves him—loves him with devotion which comes from a consciousness that she can confer

Reprinted from *Shakspere: A Critical Study of His Mind and Art* (New York, 1881), pp. 75–80. Title supplied by the present editor.

much; and she will form him so that one day she shall like him also.

 Hel. 'Tis pity.
 Parol. What's pity?
 Hel. That wishing well had not a body in't,
Which might be felt; that we, the poorer born,
Whose baser stars do shut us up in wishes,
Might with effects of them follow our friends,
And show what we alone must think.

But the "wishing well" of such a woman as Helena has indeed a sensible and apprehensible body in it. With a sacred boldness she assumes a command over Bertram's fate and her own. She cannot believe in the piety of resignation or passiveness, in the religious duty of letting things drift; rather, she finds in the love which prompts her a true mandate from above, and a veritable providential power:

 Our remedies oft in ourselves do lie
 Which we ascribe to heaven: the fated sky
 Gives us free scope, only doth backward pull
 Our slow designs when we ourselves are dull.
 What power is it that mounts my love so high?

Helena goes forth, encouraged by her mistress, the mother of the man she seeks to win; goes forth to gain her husband, to allay her own need of service to him, to impose herself on Bertram as the blessing that he requires. All this Helena does openly, with perfect courage. She does not conceal her love from the Countess; she does not for a moment dream of stealing after Bertram in man's attire. It is the most impulsively or the most delicately and exquisitely feminine of Shakspere's women whom he delights to disguise in the "garnish of a boy"—Julia, with her hair knit up "in twenty odd-conceited true-love knots"; Rosalind, the gallant curtle-axe upon her thigh; Viola, the sweet-voiced, in whom "all is semblative a woman's part"; Jessica, for whose transformation Cupid himself would blush; Portia, the wise young judge, so poignantly feminine in her gifts of intellect and heart; Imogen, who steps into the cavern's mouth with the advanced sword in a slender and trembling hand. In Helena

there is so much solidity and strength of character that we feel she would be enfeebled by any male disguise which might complicate the impression produced by her plain womanhood. There could be no charm in presenting as a pretender to male courage one who was actually courageous as a man.

But throughout, while Helena is abundantly courageous, Shakspere intends that she shall at no moment appear unwomanly. In offering herself to Bertram, she first discloses her real feeling by words addressed to one of the young lords, from among whom it is granted her to choose a husband:

 Be not afraid that I your hand should take;
 I'll never do you wrong for your own sake.

Only with Bertram she would venture on the bold experiment of wronging him for his own sake. The experiment, indeed, does not at first seem to succeed. Helena is wedded to Bertram; she has laid her will without reserve in her husband's hands; she had desired to surrender all to him, for his good, and she has surrendered all. But Bertram does not find this providential superintendence of his affairs of the heart altogether to his taste; and in company with Parolles he flies from his wife's presence to the Italian war. Upon reading the concise and cruel letter in which Bertram has declared the finality of his separation from her, Helena does not faint, nor does she break forth into bitter lamentation. "This is a dreadful sentence," " 'Tis bitter." Thus, pruning her words, Helena controls "the thoughts which swell and throng" over her, until they condense themselves into one strong purpose. She will leave her mother, leave her home; and when she is gone and forgotten, Bertram will return from hardship and danger. But she would fain see him; and if anything can still be done, she will do that thing.

The mode by which Helena succeeds in accomplishing the conditions upon which Bertram has promised to acknowledge her as his wife seems indeed hardly to possess any moral force, any validity for the heart or the conscience. It can only be said, in explanation, that to Helena an infinite virtue and significance resides in a *deed*. Out of a word or out of a feeling she does not hope for measureless good to come; but out of a deed, what may not come? That Bertram should actually have received her as his wife, actually, though unwittingly; that he should indeed be father of the child she bears him—these are facts, accomplished things, which must work out some real advantage. And now Bertram has learned his need of self-distrust, perhaps has learned true modesty. His friend (who was all vain words apart from deeds) has been unmasked and pitilessly exposed. May not Bertram now be capable of estimating the worth of things and of persons more justly? Helena, in taking the place of Diana, in beguiling her husband into at least material virtue, is still "doing him wrong, for his own sake." The man is "at woman's command," and there is "no hurt done."

Even at the last, Bertram's attainment is but small; he is still no more than a potential piece of worthy manhood. We cannot suppose that Shakspere has represented him thus without a purpose. Does not the poet wish us to feel that although much remains to be wrought in Bertram, his welfare is now assured? The courageous title of the play, *All's Well that Ends Well*, is like an utterance of the heart of Helena, who has strength and endurance to attain the end, and who will measure things, not by the pains and trials of the way, not by the dubious and difficult means, but by that end, by the accomplished issue. We need not, therefore, concern ourselves any longer about Bertram; he is safe in the hands of Helena; she will fashion him as he should be fashioned. Bertram is at length delivered from the snares and delusions which beset his years of haughty ignorance and dulness of the heart; he is doubly won by Helena; therefore he cannot wander far, therefore he cannot finally be lost.

E. K. Chambers

All's Well that Ends Well

A RATHER fantastic desire to identify *All's Well that Ends Well* with the *Love's Labour's Won* mentioned by Francis Meres is mainly responsible for the persistent attempt of many scholars to trace in its occasional rhymed passages the survivals of an earlier and discarded version of the play. But Shakespeare's use of rhyme, after he had given it up as a normal vehicle of dialogue, is apt to be deliberate, serving to indicate a heightening of the dramatic mood or to fulfil some other quite definite purpose; and it becomes in consequence a very untrustworthy guide in determining questions of chronology. There is no reason to suppose that *All's Well that Ends Well* affords an exception; and in any case, even if an earlier draft lie concealed, there can be little doubt that the whole structure and handling of the play in its present form belong to the same and to a fairly advanced date in Shakespeare's development. It groups itself undeniably with *Troilus and Cressida* and *Measure for Measure,* as one of the bitter comedies; for it is a comedy from which all laughter has evaporated, save the grim laughter which follows the dubious sallies of Monsieur Lavache and the contemptuous laughter which presides over the plucking bare of the ineffable Parolles. The spiritual affinities of Helena's story are indeed far less with the radiant humour of *Twelfth Night* and *As You Like It* than with the analytic psychology of the great advance-guard of tragedy, *Julius Caesar* and *Hamlet,* which was almost contemporary with these. Of *Hamlet* in particular, one is again and again reminded. The advice of the Countess to Bertram in the opening scene curiously re-echoes that of Polonius to Bertram's counterpart, Laertes; and what is Parolles but the more elaborate portrait of the same type of human vanity which is represented by the thumb-nail sketch of Osric the water-fly? The analogy to be traced, however, goes far deeper than this. In Brutus and in Hamlet, Shakespeare had set side by side two tragic studies of greatness failing to be greatness through the excess or defect of certain qualities whose perfect balance is necessary to efficiency. It is precisely such another study that the fortunes of Helena, if rightly read, reveal.

Like all the difficult plays, *All's Well that Ends Well* was bound to mislead the more superficial commentators. Over Helena sentiment has run riot. Hear how Mrs Jameson gushes—

There never was, perhaps, a more beautiful picture of a woman's love, cherished in secret, not self-consuming in silent languishment—not pining in thought—not passive and "desponding over its idol"—but patient and hopeful, strong in its own intensity, and sustained by its own fond faith. . . . The mere pride of rank and birth is a prejudice of which she cannot comprehend the force, because her mind towers so immeasurably above it; and, compared to the infinite love which swells within her own bosom, it sinks into nothing. She cannot conceive that he to whom she has devoted her heart and truth, her soul, her life, her services, must not one day love her in return; and once her own beyond the reach of fate, that her cares, her caresses, her unwearied, patient tenderness, will not at last "win her lord to look upon her". . . . It is this fond faith which, hoping all things, enables her to endure all things; which hallows and dignifies the surrender of her woman's pride, making it a sacrifice on which virtue and love throw a mingled incense.

Reprinted from *Shakespeare: A Survey* (London, 1925, pp. 200–07, by permission of The Macmillan Company.

One would hardly gather from this rhapsody the simple truth that the play is drenched in irony; and that what in virtue of her "fond faith" and her "unwearied, patient tenderness" Helena really effects is, firstly, to drive a man, who not merely does not love her but loves someone else, into a forced marriage by a trick, and then by another trick to substitute herself in her husband's bed for the mistress whom he wishes to seduce, and so to obtain the consummation which his not unnatural coldness would otherwise have denied her. Surely this unsavoury adventure, for the sake of a not very desirable prize, is inadequately described as "the surrender of her woman's pride."

Obviously, I think, the issue of the thing is not Helena's triumph but Helena's degradation. I conceive Shakespeare's design to have been something like this. He has shown noble manhood made ineffective as a practical instrument for life, in Hamlet by very intellect, and in Brutus by very idealism. He will now show noble womanhood made equally ineffective by the highest quality of womanhood itself, which is love; by the imperious instinct of sex, which drives Helena through unworthy paths to a profitless goal, and turns man's tender helpmate, like Mr Bernard Shaw's Anne Whitefield, into the keen and unswerving huntress of man. Thus indeed is she Dian's maid. The play will bear closer analysis from this point of view. Certainly Helena is a nobly planned woman. Her level brain, her depth of feeling, her easy mastery of every situation in which she finds herself, place her of all Shakespeare's heroines nearest to the Portia of *The Merchant of Venice*. Thus she impresses everyone with whom she comes into contact and who is competent to judge. She is the worthy child of a worthy father. "She derives her honesty and achieves her goodness." To the gracious old Countess she is dear as a daughter. "She may lawfully make title to as much love as she finds; there is more owing her than is paid, and more shall be paid her than she'll demand." To Lafeu, experienced and sane in judgment, for all his light deliverance, she is—

> One, that in her sex, her years, profession,
> Wisdom and constancy, hath amazed me more
> Than I dare blame my weakness.

To the dying king, after his first conversation with her, it seems that—

> All that life can rate
> Worth name of life, in thee hath estimate,
> Youth, beauty, wisdom, courage, all
> That happiness and prime can happy call.

Only Parolles the witless and Bertram the unseeing fail to recognize the charm and the strength that are in her. Even beyond Portia she is dowered with an indomitable will, a will that exactly measures its means to its ends and regards no obstacles in its direct advance to the achievement it has set itself. In the very first scene her judgment of character is shown by her treatment of Parolles, with whose equivocal conversation she plays as if he were a child, while her mind is set on other things. She has no doubt whatever about him, knows him a notorious liar, thinks him a great way fool, solely a coward. But Bertram she loves, and cannot judge him at all. This unequalled virgin has fallen in love with a good-looking boy, as any other woman might. Her passion lingers on his arched brows, his hawking eye, his curls. She has come to think him desirable, and herself unworthy of him. She has forgot her father—

> My imagination
> Carries no favour in it but Bertram's.
> I am undone; there is no living, none,
> If Bertram be away. It were all one
> That I should love a bright particular star,
> And think to wed it, he is so above me.

As a matter of fact, of course, Bertram is a young ass, and has shown no touch of any quality worthy to mate with Helena's save the spirit which makes him unwilling to stay at court while others go to the wars—

Creaking his shoes on the plain masonry,
Till honour be bought up, and no sword worn
But one to dance with!

The weakness of his nature is apparent in the influence won over him by Parolles, an emptyheaded and boastful fool, with just enough intelligence to make his profit out of the novice to whom he has attached himself. Parolles chooses to treat Helena as a waiting-maid, and his pupil is not likely to lay aside the insolence of birth and to recognize how far a poor physician's daughter has the advantage of him in all the gifts of head and heart. He does not improve by acquaintance. The wisdom of the king in desiring to keep him from following the wars soon becomes apparent when he reaches Florence. He does honourable service in the field, but he has no power of self-restraint, and under the apt guidance of his ring-carrier he shows himself a dangerous and lascivious boy, and a whale to virginity. Ultimately he proves even worse than this, and in the last ordeal, when he is confronted with Diana and the rings, stands confessed a cur and a liar.

It is not for long that Helena continues in the mood of self-depreciation which leads her to think Bertram out of her sphere. Even while she is talking to Parolles she realizes the strength of her own love and of her own will, and before the end of the scene her resolution is taken. Henceforward she dominates the play, and passes from dishonour to dishonour on the path to her final victory—

Our remedies oft in ourselves do lie
Which we ascribe to heaven. The fated sky
Gives us free scope; only doth backward pull
Our slow designs when we ourselves are dull.

The first remedy is clearly to follow Bertram to Paris, and so she lies glibly and with an air of extreme candour to the Countess, and leaves behind her the impression that the only motive of her journey is the hope of curing the king. The king is cured, and Helena, who has been careful to secure the promise of her reward before-hand, claims Bertram's hand. There is a pretty air of modest deference about her—

I dare not say I take you; but I give
Me and my service, ever whilst I live,
Into your guiding power.

Nevertheless she does take him, standing by cool and self-possessed, while the grateful king forces her hand upon a most reluctant husband. Even young asses have their rights, and one cannot but feel some sympathy with Bertram, who, as it appears afterwards, has already cast his eyes on Maudlin Lafeu, when he bursts out with his—

O my Parolles, they have married me!

After the ceremony he dismisses Helena briefly enough. She is reduced to beg a kiss, which is denied her; and with this humiliation makes her way to Roussillon. Here she learns that it is his intention never to bed her, and at the thought of him in the wars her first instinct is to relent and set him free. But will is elastic and reasserts itself. She lies again to the Countess in the letter which expresses her intention to go upon a pilgrimage, so that Bertram may return; for, although she does put on the palmer's garb, it is only to pursue her husband to Florence. Here occurs the substitution incident which, in this play as in *Measure for Measure*, proves a difficult morsel for the sentimental reader. Mrs Jameson faces the problem by saying that "the circumstances and details with which Helena is surrounded are shocking to our feelings and wounding to our delicacy; and yet the beauty of the character is made to triumph over all." Of course that is not really so. The meanness of the device to which Helena stoops in order to secure a nominal possession of her husband is a measure of the spiritual straits to which the instinct of sex has reduced the noblest of women. Then come more lies, growing easier and easier each time, until she can shepherd Bertram with the report of her death back to Marseilles, and there claim him in the presence of the king by a proof of the literal fulfilment of the conditions he had laid down.

In the end Bertram is reconciled. He has already outgrown the "snipped-taffeta fellow" and "red-tailed humble-bee" Parolles, and perhaps Helena may succeed in making a man of him some day. But after all it is a poor prize for which she has trailed her honour in the dust; and comedy has made strange progress with Shakespeare since he shook our sides at the gross roguery of Falstaff, or even the befooling of the poor coxcomb Malvolio. Behind comedy so unsmiling as this some perturbation of the once sunny spirit must needs lie.

Hazelton Spencer

All's Well that Ends Well

IF Shakespeare had not sent Bertram and Helena to bed together, there would be no compelling reason against the inclusion of this play among the romantic comedies or the dramatic romances; and "shocking," "revolting," and "corrupt" might have lain dormant in the vocabularies of its critics. Despite the substantial difference between that odd nuptial couch and the veil of decorum in the joyous comedies, it is possible to exaggerate the bedlessness of the earlier plays. Their heroines are sweet and pure, but not cold. Like Helena, they sometimes converse with a frankness unknown to the "nice girl" of Victorian convention. Lysander proposes to pass the night on the same pillow; and Hermia, though she loves him, insists on

> Such separation as may well be said
> Becomes a virtuous bachelor and a maid.

Portia hears Gratiano's broadest witticism, and it is not nominated in the score that the pearl of heroines is offended by it. She is herself afterwards remarkably pleasant on the privileges she expects to grant the wearer of a certain ring. The merry Beatrice goes out of her way to protest that though she has just "put down" Benedick he shall not do the same by her, lest she "prove the mother of fools"—as if there could be any danger of that! Rosalind is playful with her Orlando on "your wive's wit going to your neighbour's bed." Of them all Viola is most devoured by "the terrible lion of loving"; she is never in a mood to jest about love. She burns with a steadfast flame of passion so intense, and she is so pierced with her double sorrow, that her mind is far too occupied as well as too pure to anticipate connubial joys with sensual imagery.

Yet the bed trick in *All's Well* and in *Measure for Measure* has thrown many an unhistorically minded critic into curious fits. To the Elizabethans, we may be sure, there seemed nothing immodest about it, especially since the condition was imposed on Helena by her husband, and in *Measure for Measure* is suggested by the virtuous Duke. In both dramas, the trick is played by a wronged woman whose affection has remained unaltered. By means of it Helena's marriage to the man she loves is consummated; it is a brilliant marriage for her and a lucky one for him. It was in a later age, when the old romances were no longer human nature's daily food, that it occurred to anyone to question whether the ending is really a happy one. The convention under which Shakespeare was writing prescribed, and still prescribes in fiction designed for the unsophisticated, that when the thing ends on the right joyous note, whether of happy bells or of Mendelssohn's march or of a long kiss that symbolizes them, the story is over. Certainly there is no trace of irony or scepticism in Shakespeare's handling of this very romantic plot. . . .

To modern readers Bertram's character has been the great stumbling block, but that is inherent in the plot, if we are to be wholeheartedly for Helena. Shakespeare means that we shall be, and so he makes Bertram stupid and even vicious in his rejection of her, although in Boccaccio he is neither and his motive is the understandable one of aversion to a marriage beneath his rank. Helena, noble creature that she is, needs not in the eyes of this generation the defense which, despite the admiration of Coleridge and Hazlitt, had till quite recently to be put up for her. She is utterly without and above feminine artifice. The methods by which she backs the skittish Bertram between the thrills of matrimony are, like her dangerous ministry to the King, more intellectual than temperamental, more boldly masculine than reliant on the wiles of sex. She employs no lures, no coquetries; she does not try either to dazzle or to enchant; she refrains from turning on the full force of her charm. But before the first scene is half over she has won our sympathy completely by her passionate reckless soliloquy of desperate love:—"I think not on my father," though we are confident she loved him deeply:

> What was he like?
> I have forgot him. My imagination
> Carries no favour in't but Bertram's.
> I am undone! There is no living, none,
> If Bertram be away.

Her conduct throughout is, for a heroine of old romance, in complete harmony with this declaration. Hers is a love like Viola's, and it carries her even farther—in miles and in expedients. So she goes to Paris; but when her great moment comes, only to shame her, and Bertram roundly replies, "I cannot love her, nor will strive to do't," she wins us all the more by her dignity in pain:

> That you are well restor'd, my lord, I'm glad.
> Let the rest go.

Shakespeare is artful for her. It is the King who presses the reluctant youth, not she. After that come solemn oaths and an awful sanction, and she has, according to the older view of such matters, not only rights but duties. That the King should dictate a marriage is not in the least surprising; it was a commonplace in life as well as in fiction. That it was, makes Helena's choice of a reward still less open to objection.

As for Bertram, if he had recognized his happiness when it met him, there would be no play. He is even more obtuse than Orsino, whom we prefer because he speaks poetry. But Bertram was not, presumably, a hateful specimen to the Elizabethans. He is immature; he is misguided by Parolles; he makes mistakes of his own. He sees the light at the end very suddenly—as men sometimes do in real life, as is customary in romantic plots that wind up with a change of heart (it is no less abrupt in Boccaccio), as is more or less necessary in a play that must conform to a strict time limit, and as is more acceptable in a drama than in other forms of fiction because an audience *witnesses* the hero's revulsion of feeling and in the theatre seeing is believing, provided the acting is all it should be. The unexpected appearance of the woman he has injured shocks Bertram, we must suppose, out of his wayward humor into his true self; and with his eager promise to love her "ever, ever dearly" Shakespeare's audience was doubtless completely satisfied.

If we are not, even after making the historical discount, the reason is probably the scarcity of poetry. This may be due to haste or some lack of interest; it is probably not the result of the author's having gone sour. Mere style, when it drips from Shakespeare's pen, can create the romantic haze or fairy mist through which an absurd plot will loom up as inevitable. As usual, he is telling a story. In this comedy he tells little else. And he does not tell it with his usual charm. *All's Well* transports us no farther than along the beaten tracks of France and Italy; we touch at no Illyrian shore, we wander in no Arden glades. Instead of a languishing Duke all "canopied with bow'rs," or a composer of verses published by the trees of the forest, or any of the other young lovers who succeed in being gloriously ardent without kissing, we have for hero a boy aristocrat as ambitious as they come and hard with the hardness of the youngster who has yet both to win his spurs and to prove himself with women. He takes to war as to his native element; and he assumes, like any young blood without a poetic side, that one learns what women are by commencing rake. Bertram, in contrast with the lovers of the romantic comedies, provides an additional warrant for calling this one, at least relatively, realistic. Neither his blindness nor his attempt on Diana endear him, yet it is hard to see why he should be singled out for universal denunciation. *All's Well* is not a recent work, and in older fiction the hero is often expected to make a few mistakes before he straightens out and settles down. Compared with the young gentlemen of the eighteenth-century novel, Bertram is, save of course for a deficiency of sensibility, almost a model youth. It is perhaps regrettable that Shakespeare failed to invent some scene in which the recreant husband might help an old lady across the street or throw his purse to a deserving beggar or perform some other good turn that would prove him the owner of a heart of gold at least the equal of Tom Jones's. Aptitude for war, however, went a long way toward establishing a romantic hero. He is, moreover, a count and a protégé of the King of France. He does the right thing in the end. The play's title clinches the argument against its detractors.

To be sure, no one is obliged to like it. But if one can bring oneself to accept the romantic plot, the effort is worth making, for the play repays reading. It is a little thin, as Elizabethan dramas go, there being no subplot, unless we count the exposure of Parolles. But its tone, while not gay, is not depressing; on the contrary, it is lofty and exhilarating. The absurdity of calling it sordid becomes obvious with the reflection that every one of the feminine characters is decent through and through. Two of them are very noble women—not Helena alone, for the Countess is fully her equal, a great lady and a true lady, as charming old Lafew is the true gentleman. Lavatch is not among the greatest of the clowns; he is coarser and less merry, but his wit comes from the same mint. Like Feste, he is perfectly sane and a jester by profession. Parolles is a variation on that familiar theme, the braggart captain—and what a variation! One might think that by this time Shakespeare and Jonson, to mention no others, had put this veteran figure through all possible comic hoops; but Parolles, however he marches to the wars in the column that stretches back through the *commedia dell' arte* to the ancient comedy of Rome, and however he is like Pistol in his poltroonery and his complete innocence of the saving grace of humor, is not Pistol. He is Parolles. Each is unique; each speaks his own language. Parolles was "dressed," of course, in the most extravagant costume the wardrobe afforded. Before he spoke a word, his first entrance doubtless raised a mighty laugh, in which, if he so elects, the reader is still privileged to join.

Harold S. Wilson

Dramatic Emphasis in *All's Well that Ends Well*

. . . Among all the various objections that have been lodged against the improbabilities of the action, the inconsistency of the heroine and the moral baseness of the hero, the coarseness of the dialogue and the poor quality of the verse, the most specific seem to be the charges of inconsistency or implausibility directed against the heroine and the hero, especially in the climax of the action. Nowadays, particularly in view of Professor Lawrence's argument,[1] we may grant Shakespeare his premises for the play: that there is nothing immodest about the means Helena uses to win back her husband. This is insisted upon by the dramatist himself, in the attitude Diana and her mother take to Helena's proposals. If we object to the play because of the "bed-trick," we reject the story itself, regardless of the execution. But it is argued that even granting the premises of the folktale which provides the action of the play (Shakespeare fails to make his heroine consistently appealing) that he creates an artificial climax which offends against all probability; and that the conversion of Bertram at the end is sudden and unconvincing: that he remains odious to the last.

These are undeniably weak points of the play that are most readily apparent to a reader. But if we compare *All's Well* with its source, we may observe that these difficulties are attributable not to Boccaccio's story but to the changes Shakespeare made in it. It is arguable that Shakespeare deliberately incurred the difficulties alleged in an attempt to transform a simple tale of

reconciliation effected through circumstance into a study of character; and that he used a method of shifting emphasis to obscure the implausibilities resulting from his treatment of his source and calculated to give a sufficient unity of effect in stage performance.

It will be necessary to examine briefly Shakespeare's treatment of his source, to substantiate the first part of this argument before we turn to the second.

Boccaccio's tale of Giletta of Narbonne, in William Painter's faithful translation,[2] furnished the plot of *All's Well*. It is a folktale by a master of rapid narrative with the simplicity and emphasis upon action to the disregard of motivation or psychological probability that is characteristic of the kind.

Giletta is a clever girl of humble birth, with respect to the hero, the Count Beltramo of Rossiglione, whom she loves devotedly and seemingly hopelessly. As the daughter of a famous physician, however, she is able to heal the French king of an apparently incurable disease and as her reward chooses Beltramo as a husband. The Count scorns her humble birth, and the King himself regards her choice as presumptuous, though he feels bound to support it. Beltramo deserts his newly married bride for the Florentine wars, while Giletta returns to Rossiglione, where she learns from the Count's letters that he will not consent to live with her until she can get a ring from his finger and has a child of his begetting in her arms. Giletta goes to Florence with the purpose of finding some means to fulfill the conditions. There she learns that Beltramo is trying to seduce the virtuous daughter of a poor gentlewoman. Giletta

---

[1] The reference is to the discussion of *All's Well* in W. W. Lawrence's *Shakespeare's Problem Comedies* (New York, 1931), pp. 32 ff. [Ed.]

[2] In the *Decameron*, it is the ninth story of the third day. Painter's translation may be consulted in *The Palace of Pleasure*, ed. Joseph Jacobs (London, 1890), I, 171–79.

Reprinted by permission from the *Huntington Library Quarterly*, XIII (May 1950), 222–40.

proposes that the daughter should seem to encourage Beltramo's advances, demanding his ring as a pledge, and that Giletta herself should take the daughter's place in bed. The mother, willing to help the lady recover her husband, secretly arranges matters so that Giletta obtains the ring and is soon with child. Beltramo returns to Rossiglione at the request of his subjects, knowing that his wife is no longer there. Giletta richly rewards the gentlewoman and her daughter, who retire to the country. Giletta herself stays in Florence until she is delivered of twin boys, who are carefully nursed; at length she learns that her husband is giving a great feast at his palace on All Saint's Day to an assembly of ladies and knights. As the guests are about to sit down, Giletta appears before Beltramo with her two sons in her arms, falls weeping at his feet, and pleads that since his conditions have now been fulfilled she may be accepted as his wife. All the assembled guests join in her plea, and the Count, much moved, "abiected his obstinate rigour: causing her to rise vp, and imbraced and kissed her, acknowledging her againe for his lawefull wyfe . . . and from that time forth, hee loued and honoured her, as his dere spouse and wyfe."

In this story we learn little or nothing of the heroine's feelings and we infer her character simply from her actions. We do not hear how she felt when Beltramo deserted her for the Florentine wars, though we are told what she did: she set about putting his estate in order, hoping thus to win his approval. Two knights report to her Beltramo's conditions for accepting her as his wife: "who, very sorrowfull, after shee had a good while bethoughte her, purposed to finde meanes to attaine the two thinges, that thereby she might recouer her husbande." Giletta is the most active of heroines; she does not waste time on sentiment but goes straight to work. She is consistently active and the center of interest in the action throughout.

The Count Beltramo is likewise a very satisfactory hero for a folk-tale. His initial rejection of Giletta is well motivated by the disparity in their rank, which everyone, including the King, recognizes. While the conditions he imposes are very difficult, no one makes any great point of their harshness;

and he is so slightly drawn that we hardly notice how his adulterous intentions reflect upon his character. He is a great lord, and these are his lordly ways. His conduct at the end is everything one could wish: he is warm-hearted and generous in his acceptance of Giletta, "and they lived happily ever after."

The burden of justification falls upon Giletta throughout Boccaccio's story. She is the Clever Wench of folklore, as Professor Lawrence has shown, who wins a husband of exalted rank through performing one difficult task, and then has to maintain her right to her reward through performing two more. Her husband provides the occasion of all three tasks, and he rewards her successful achievement. The appeal of the story lies in the working out of the plot, and there is no attempt to complicate it with considerations of the relative merits of hero and heroine. The outcome assumes that the heroine's virtue is sufficiently rewarded when she is at last accepted by the Count.

Shakespeare followed the main lines of Boccaccio's excellent plot, but he elaborated it with background and atmosphere, with heightened dramatic conflict, especially in the climax, and above all with the study of character. He provided the Roussillon setting—the charming old Countess, the Clown, and Lafeu; Bertram's vainglorious supporter Parolles and the sub-plot of his unmasking as a coward; and the complications of Bertram's confrontation by Diana with a second ring at the end. But the change that affected all the rest was in the characterization of the hero and heroine. He chose to make of Bertram a rash and arrogant youth who cruelly repulses a Helena who

> deserves a lord
> That twenty such rude boys might wait upon
> And call her hourly mistress.

Shakespeare thus in effect reverses the relation between hero and heroine in the source, places the main emphasis of his story upon the nobility of the heroine in her affliction, and makes necessary the repentance of Bertram to reward Helena in the end.[3] These changes create a problem of consistency regarding the heroine and of motivation concerning the hero. Shakespeare ran the risk of involving himself in contradiction when he attempted to make Helena more dramatically appealing than the original story allowed for, when he emphasized her superiority to the hero, her noble humility and pathos, while her conduct remained that of Boccaccio's Giletta who has little of this appeal. In the first part of the action, while things are going against the heroine, there is no difficulty; but when Helena becomes the effective architect of her own success in the second part, the danger is that while the Helena of "The Healing of the King" episode (to use Professor Lawrence's analysis of the plot) may seem to be a figure "touched with the most soul-subduing pathos," as Mrs. Jameson has it,[4] the Helena of "The Fulfillment of the Tasks" becomes a Clever Wench bent upon getting her man. At the same time, there is the problem of adequately prompting Bertram's reform at the end of the second episode, in harmonious relation with Helena's operations.

[3] Professor Lawrence argues that Shakespeare's audience would not regard the disparity in rank between Bertram and Helena as sufficient ground for Bertram's repulse of her, as would the courtly audience pictured in the *Decameron*; whereas the Elizabethans *would* take a sterner view of the hero's adulterous intentions; and that therefore Shakespeare was obliged to degrade the character whom Boccaccio had represented as a good fellow and quite a satisfactory husband for the heroine (*Shakespeare's Problem Comedies*, pp. 59–62). But one finds far more wayward and arrogant husbands than Bertram, who yet prove acceptable enough in the end, in . . . [other Elizabethan plays]; and for a hero of Bertram's own rank, whose adulterous intentions are easily overlooked in the end, we may compare the Count Hippolito in Dekker's *Honest Whore, Part II*. The simpler explanation of the degrading of Bertram in *All's Well* is that this provides the chief means of developing the virtue and appeal of the heroine, which is the central theme of the play.

[4] *Shakespeare's Heroines* (London, 1897), p. 108. Mrs. Jameson, of course, finds no inconsistency in Helena.

It is the means by which Shakespeare deals with these difficulties in terms of a stage performance with which the present paper is concerned. Briefly, the argument will be this: Shakespeare sets Helena before us in the first stage of the action as a nobly-loving woman who suffers Bertram's injustice with moving humility and unselfish devotion, though the emphasis upon her virtue is never overdone. The second part of the story requires her to act with a calculating initiative and successful resource that threatens to rob her of our sympathy. At this danger point in the action, Helena, to whom our allegiance is now fully engaged, ceases to be the center of attention in the developing action. The Florentine widow and her daughter Diana, Parolles and his unmasking as a coward, the ordeal of Bertram at Roussillon, successively provide the focus of interest, while Helena works out her designs unobtrusively in the background. Diana becomes an *alter ego* for Helena in executing her bolder operations, while our original impression of the heroine is maintained by the attitude of the other characters toward her and what they say of her; it is the *idea* of Helena that sustains our impression of the consistency of her character in the second episode, up to the moment when she reappears in her old role of the humble and devoted wife.

As the emphasis moves from Helena midway in the play, it centers increasingly upon the preparation for the breakdown and conversion of Bertram in the climax—through the implications of the Parolles sub-plot and the dramatization of Bertram's ordeal at Roussillon prior to Helena's reappearance. At that dramatic moment, our attention is engaged by Helena; and Bertram's repentance has been sufficiently prepared for that his capitulation seems but the proper tribute to her nobility, as we witness the happy union of a reformed hero with a heroine whose humble devotion has never changed.

A review of the action of the play will attempt to make this clear.

It is a humble and dejected Helena whom we meet in the opening scene of the play, as Bertram leaves for the Parisian court; and this impression is confirmed in her first soliloquy, where we learn that her tears are for Bertram and the hopelessness of her love:

There is no living, none,
If Bertram be away. 'Twere all one
That I should love a bright particular star
And think to wed it, he is so above me.

But her spirit immediately shows in her following encounter with Parolles, whom she perfectly recognizes for what he is, "a notorious liar . . . a great way fool, solely a coward," and yet is willing to love because he is Bertram's companion. Like the cheap swaggerer he is, Parolles tries to tease her with his coarse jests upon virginity; but she goodhumoredly parries his jibes and adroitly turns the tables on him by covertly hinting at his lack of the military virtue he professes, until, as he bustles back and forth, he is so ludicrously at a loss for a sufficient retort that he splutters, "I am so full of businesses, I cannot answer thee acutely." Clearly, if Helena is humble and loving, she is also a girl of wit and spirit. The delicate balance of her character is thus deftly fixed at the beginning.

After Parolles leaves, as if Helena's bout with him had been enough to rally her spirits, we see her forming resolve, in her second soliloquy, as the idea of healing the King and thus winning her love first occurs to her.

The second scene pictures Bertram's reception at court. The King pronounces an eloquent eulogy upon Bertram's father, emphasizing especially his modesty, courtesy, and judgment; and we are prepared by the King's:

Youth, thou bear'st thy father's face.
Frank nature, rather curious than in haste,
Hath well compos'd thee. Thy father's moral parts
May'st thou inherit too!

to mark the contrast of Bertram's rash arrogance a little later. The Countess has already described him to Lafeu as an unseasoned courtier, and the companionship of Parolles speaks eloquently of his untried judgment.

In the third scene we return to Roussillon, where the Countess learns of Helena's love for her son. The conflict in Helena between her love for Bertram and her sense of the presumption of such a love, issuing in an agonized uncertainty, would be enough to win our sympathy. Nothing could be finer than the old Countess's understanding of Helena's feelings, her sure tact in eliciting the girl's confession, and her warm support of her, once she understands Helena's plan. We learn to respect Helena partly through the Countess's faith in her, and we see suggested in the older woman's gentleness and wisdom the sort of matron that Helena may eventually become. There is further the hint that Heaven looks with favor upon Helena's attempt, as she buoyantly concludes,

There's something in't
More than my father's skill, which was the greatest
Of his profession, that his good receipt
Shall for my legacy be sanctified
By the luckiest stars in heaven.

The upward movement of Act I points toward Helena's success; but the odds against her are so uncertain as only to enlist our sympathies on her behalf without foreshadowing the outcome. Helena's triumphant healing of the King in Act II is immediately followed by the dramatic reversal of her rejection by Bertram. Helena is the center of attention in every scene except the second, in which the Countess jests with the Clown and despatches him with letters to Paris—a necessary interlude to allow time for Helena's cure to work upon the King. The developing action shows the irony of Helena's success: she heals the King, only to be scorned by the husband she wins, to be packed off to Roussillon again while Bertram deserts her for the Florentine wars. This falling movement develops the pathos of Helena, for the main emphasis falls upon her loving submissiveness and humility in defeat.

The high point of Helena's appeal comes in the second scene of Act III, after her return to Roussillon, where she receives the letter containing Bertram's conditions:

When thou canst get the ring upon my finger which shall never come off, and show me a child begotten of thy body that I am father to, then call me husband; but in such a "then" I write a "never."

"Here is my passport," she says, as she hands the letter to the Countess; "this is a dreadful sentence." A little later, she adds, " 'Tis bitter." Nothing more. The Countess hotly blames her son; but not Helena.[5] When she is left alone, we learn the thoughts that are passing in her mind. She would spare Bertram the dangers of war and restore to him the position of which her presumption has deprived him. She does not criticize him; she does not offer herself even the consolation of regarding her own intended departure from Roussillon as a sacrifice. She does not think of herself at all, but only of Bertram's welfare:

> I will be gone.
> My being here it is that holds thee hence.
> Shall I stay here to do't? No, no, although
> The air of paradise did fan the house
> And angels offic'd all. I will be gone,
> That pitiful rumour may report my flight
> To consolate thine ear. Come, night; end, day.
> For with the dark, poor thief, I'll steal away.

Thus Shakespeare shows us what it would be like if love were perfect in humility. The effect of such a virtue can be easily over-

done. In *How A Man May Choose A Good Wife From A Bad*,[6] Mistress Arthur's wayward husband repeatedly insults his wife in public, beats her, brings home a courtesan whom he prefers to his wife's place at table amid his guests. All this she bears without the least complaint. Finally he attempts to poison her, that he may marry the courtesan. Yet when the long-suffering Mistress Arthur is rescued by her husband's rival for her affections, who sums up the tale of her husband's offences ending with the report that he has now married the courtesan, thinking his wife dead, she replies to his demand, "And can you love him yet?" with

> And yet, and yet, and still, and euer whilst I
>   breathe this ayre:
> Nay after death my vnsubstantiall soule,
> Like a good Angell shall attend on him,
> And keepe him from all harme.
> But is he married, much good do his heart,
> Pray God she may content him better farre
> Then I haue done: long may they liue in peace,
> Till *I* disturbe their solace; but because
> I feare some mischiefe doth hang ore his head,
> Ile weep mine eyes drie with my present care,
> And for their healths make hoarce my toong
>   with praier.

Upon which sentiment another character comments, with perhaps unintentional irony,

> Art sure she is a woman? if she be,
> She is create of Natures puritie.[7]

Helena's virtue is less extravagant. It is apparent more often in what she leaves unsaid, in the oblique comments of others, and in the action. It is never thrust upon us in the ingenuous vein of the moralities, and it is the more impressive because it is unobtrusive.

In Boccaccio's tale, the heroine sets out for Florence with the purpose of finding some means to fulfill her husband's conditions. Helena imposes upon herself the

---

[5] We may contrast the indignation of Imogen when she learns from Pisanio of her husband's order to put her to death for being false to his bed (*Cymbeline*, III, iv). The circumstances are not closely parallel; but some protest from Helena at Bertram's cruelty would be very natural. The careful abstaining from anything like it indicates very clearly Shakespeare's conception of her essential virtue, which is humility.

[6] See the edition of A. E. H. Swaen in Bang's *Materialien* (Louvain, 1912), volume 35.

[7] Ed. Swaen, lines 2158-71.

penance of a pilgrimage to St. Jacques' shrine for her too ambitious love; and it is thus innocently she comes to Florence, where she meets the Florentine widow and Diana because St. Jacques' pilgrims are accustomed to lodge at their house. In the scene of their encounter (III, v), every care is taken to avoid the suggestion of a design upon Bertram in Helena's behavior, and to emphasize her pathos. The Florentine women take the lead in censuring Bertram and Parolles, as they see them returning from battle, for their solicitation of Diana; and they question Helena, as a Frenchwoman, about Bertram's marriage, since they have heard but coarse reports of his lady from Parolles. "O, I believe with him," says Helena;

> In argument of praise, or to the worth
> Of the great Count himself, she is too mean
> To have her name repeated. All her deserving
> Is a reserved honesty, and that
> I have not heard examin'd.

Diana comments,

>   Alas, poor lady!
> 'Tis a hard bondage to become the wife
> Of a detesting lord.

And her mother,

> Ay, right! Good creature, wheresoe'er she is,
> Her heart weighs sadly.

By such slight touches, Shakespeare tips the scale of our sympathy. Though Helena learns the circumstances that are to provide the means of fulfilling her tasks in this scene, no hint of her forming purpose is given. She invites the Florentine women to dinner and promises to bestow some precepts on Diana "worthy the note." And we turn to the affairs of Bertram and Parolles.

The action which takes place in Florence after the arrival of Helena is divided in alternate scenes between the affairs of Helena and those of Bertram and Parolles. This takes us up to the last scene of Act IV, which sets the stage for the denouement at Roussillon in Act V. But the chief dramatic interest lies in the exposure of Parolles as a coward, which unfolds as a unified sub-plot rising to a comic climax in Act IV, scene iii, while the scenes dealing with Helena's activities are much briefer and serve largely to punctuate with exposition the stages in the development of the dramatic sub-plot. After Parolles has boasted that he will recover his drum from the enemy and Bertram has been persuaded to take him at his word by the two French lords, who plan to entrap the braggart, a brief scene of forty-eight lines between Helena and the Florentine widow explains Helena's design of obtaining Bertram's ring and substituting herself for Diana; and the emphasis, in their conversation, is upon the lawfulness of Helena's purpose. Then we have the capture of Parolles, with the comic business of his terror and the jargon of his captors. The next scene is between Bertram and Diana, in which Diana obtains Bertram's ring and makes her assignation. Here Diana is spirited enough in her satirical opposition to Bertram's advances and her feigned reluctance in yielding; and she is just sufficiently realized as a character to give us the sense that she is aiding and protecting Helena against the wickedness of Bertram, rather than that she is serving as her puppet to entrap him.

The climactic scene of Parolles' exposure is the high point of Act IV, as it is the principal comic event of the play. It serves to remove the supporter of Bertram's villainy and thus to prepare for the hero's subsequent reformation. Up to this point, Bertram has been shown to us in the worst possible lights; his only extenuation has been the corrupting influence of Parolles. His faults and mistakes are severely reviewed by the two French lords as a preliminary to Parolles' exposure: Bertram "has much worthy blame laid upon him for shaking off so good a wife and so sweet a lady"; he has forfeited the King's favor by his arrogance; he is at present licentiously pursuing his amour with Diana and has had the bad taste to boast of it. But if Bertram is licentious and arrogant and indiscreet, he has nothing of the blusterer or the coward about him, and the Dumain brothers, for all their severity, think it worth their while to unmask Parolles for his benefit. If Parolles has been the encourager of Bertram's riots, he is also a foil beside whom Bertram begins to appear less base; when he sees Parolles for what he really is, a part of his education has been accomplished.

Parolles reminded Dr. Johnson of Falstaff; he has rather more in common, perhaps, with Ancient Pistol in *Henry V*. They are both men of words, swaggerers and cowards who attach themselves to military undertakings, overreach themselves through their military pretensions, and, after they have been exposed, unashamedly accept their ignominy. He has been accused of dullness: "We conceive Parolles to be . . . about the inanest of all Shakespeare's inventions," says Quiller-Couch, and goes on to abuse him for his bawdy talk to Helena in a fine burst of Victorian indignation.[8] But there is need of a distinction here. Parolles is clumsy and coarse in his attempts to impose himself, and is constantly found out. Everyone sees through him from the beginning, except Bertram. Helena is the first, in the opening of the play; later Lafeu and the Clown—all make sport of him. That Bertram does not perceive the emptiness of his airs is the clearest evidence of his youthful inexperience.

But in the great scene of his unmasking as a craven, Shakespeare chooses to kindle Parolles' imagination—as he could apparently do for his characters at will—and in the wonderful description Parolles gives of his captors, the brothers Dumain, while he is blindfolded in their presence and Bertram's, there is a fund of comic invention that reminds one of the wit-combats between Hal and Falstaff [9]—save that the wit

---

[8] *All's Well*, Cambridge ed., pp. xxiv–v.

[9] The device of mounting hyperbole for comic effect is, however, common elsewhere in the plays. One recalls Kent's character of Oswald (*Lear*, II, ii), and Imogen's emphatic rejection of the advances of Cloten (*Cym.*, II, iii) as notable examples.

---

is all on Parolles' side, and, from the unfortunate circumstances in which he finds himself, he can get no credit for his brilliance. Of one of the brothers Dumain he says,

He will steal, sir, an egg out of a cloister. For rapes and ravishments he parallels Nessus. He professes not keeping of oaths; in breaking 'em he is stronger than Hercules; he will lie, sir, with such volubility, that you would think Truth were a fool. Drunkenness is his best virtue, for he will be swine-drunk, and in his sleep he does little harm, save to his bedclothes about him; but they know his conditions and lay him in straw.

Since we have just heard the gentleman so described, in the passage immediately preceding, deliver a stern homily upon human sinfulness in general and Bertram's in particular that would grace a pulpit, the contrast is very pleasant. Parolles goes on to describe his military experience:

Faith, sir, has led the drum before the English tragedians. To belie him, I will not, and more of his soldiership I know not; except, in that country he had the honour to be the officer at a place there called Mile-end, to instruct for the doubling of files. I would do the man what honour I can, but of this I am not certain.

After a pause, no doubt for the audience to regain its equanimity after this particular stroke of local color, the second Dumain brother, whose character has not yet been touched upon, comments wonderingly: "He hath out-villain'd villainy so far, that the rarity redeems him."

But Parolles has not yet reached the summit of his rhetorical flight. "Will gold corrupt him?" asks his interlocutor. And Parolles replies:

Sir, for a *quart d'écu* he will sell the fee-simple of his salvation, the inheritance of it; and cut th'entail from all remainders, and a perpetual succession for it perpetually.

We can sympathize with the second brother, who exclaims, with alarmed chagrin, when the interlocutor asks Parolles about him, "Why does he ask him of me?" Bertram is too much involved in Parolles' humiliation to find the demonstration funny. "I could endure anything before but a cat; and now he's a cat to me," he mutters; and his sullenly reiterated "he's a cat still," shows us his increasing embarrassment.

Parolles is impertinent or abject, prominent or negligible in the action, as the dramatic situation requires. While he acts as an evil influence upon Bertram, he is just stupid enough to appear impudent and odious, just plausible enough to insinuate himself with a headstrong boy like Bertram, and no one else. But when he has served his turn as the corrupter of Bertram and needs to be shown as the figure of comedy he truly is, Shakespeare gives him his great moment, and dismisses him with one of those unforgettable speeches that sum up the soul of his being—and in him a part of universal mankind:

> Yet am I thankful. If my heart were great,
> 'Twould burst at this. Captain I'll be no more;
> But I will eat and drink, and sleep as soft
> As captain shall. Simply the thing I am
> Shall make me live.

After the exposure of Parolles, Helena further explains to the widow and Diana her purpose of bringing them to the King at Marseilles, who will vouch for her good faith and suitably reward Diana:

> Doubt not but Heaven
> Hath brought me up to be your daughter's dower,
> As it hath fated her to be my motive
> And helper to a husband.

This indirect proceeding avoids the suggestion that Helena deliberately plans to confront Bertram in the King's presence. As we learn in the opening of Act V, they reach Marseilles only to discover that the King is to be found at Roussillon. Helena sends a petition to him—the nature of which is not disclosed until later—by a gentleman of the court whom she meets, and Helena's party follows at a slower pace, still on the pretext that Helena is acting for the benefit of Diana and her mother.

Helena's is the directing mind in all these arrangements, but every suggestion serves to minimize her contrivance. The overshadowing effect of the Parolles sub-plot, Helena's brief and undramatic appearances, the activity of Diana as Helena's substitute, the suggestion that Helena is acting more on the behalf of her Florentine companions than herself, and that all their efforts are in fulfillment of the will of heaven—all of these means serve indirectly to maintain the impression of subdued pathos that is essential to the integrity of Helena's role. They serve as well, of course, to conceal the means by which the reversal is to be achieved in the climax and thus to heighten its dramatic effect. To the consideration of the technique of this climax, which has been so much criticized, we may now turn.

At Roussillon, Bertram has returned, and Helena is supposed to have died upon her pilgrimage. It is now proposed that Bertram marry Lafeu's daughter, and, as their betrothal is about to take place in the King's presence, the petition which Helena had sent on from Marseilles but which now purports to come from Diana is presented to the King. Professor Lawrence objects to the implausibility of what follows:

The obscure Florentine maiden becomes an expert stage-manager, keeping everyone in the dark as to her real purpose, boldly bandying words with the king, driving Bertram into a tight corner, and finally producing Helena, as a grand *coup de théâtre*. She has sent the king a petition, begging him to force Bertram to marry her, since, as she says, he is a widower, and he has seduced her. But Diana knows that he is not a widower and that he has not seduced her, and she has no desire to marry him. When confronted with Bertram, she plays out the same comedy, showing his ring as proof, and forcing him to dishonorable calumnies and to a confession of guilt. She then asks for her ring again. This ring has a complicated history. It has been given by the king to Helena, and then to Bertram by Helena in the night rendezvous. Bertram has earlier in this same scene offered it as a marriage-token to Maudlin, the daughter of Lafeu; it was then taken by the king, and is now on his finger. Diana knows perfectly well that it is not her ring, and the king knows it is not, for he had himself earlier given it to Helena. Bertram confesses (what he supposes to be true) that the ring belonged to Diana. The king then asks her about it, and she answers him in an intentionally riddling and misleading fashion. In anger, the king orders her off to prison. Then Diana, having extracted from the situation all the surprises it can yield, produces Helena, as her crowning stage-effect, and the play quickly ends. All this may be good drama, but it is bad psychology.[10]

But Professor Lawrence has here overlooked the circumstances which give precisely the psychological justification for Diana's behavior that he desiderates—that she is acting under Helena's direction and on her behalf, and with the purpose of bringing about Bertram's repentance. Furthermore, in his comment upon Helena's role at the end, he has surely misconceived *her* purpose and the effect which her actions are calculated to produce. The "natural way" for Helena to prove that she has fulfilled Bertram's conditions and deserves to be accepted as his wife, says Professor Lawrence, would be for her "to claim justice of the king, tell her story, and call upon Diana to substantiate it." [11] But this would be of no avail with an unrepentant Bertram; indeed, it reduces the play to the simplicity of its folk-tale source. Helena in *All's Well* is not seeking justice of the King but Bertram's love. In Boccaccio's tale, the heroine's fulfillment of the tasks is enough to win her happy union with the hero. In Shakespeare, Helena's efforts would go for nothing did not Bertram experience a change of heart. In the climax, everything is directed toward this end; and this is the abundant psychological justification of the means used, for Bertram is still far from penitent as we see him in the opening of the last scene.

There has been some preparation for Bertram's conversion. We have seen his disillusionment about Parolles. The news of Helena's death has sobered him too, and

10 *Shakespeare's Problem Comedies*, pp. 75–76.
11 *Ibid.*, p. 75.

he professes to have learned to love her now that he has lost her, while the preliminary arrangements for his betrothal to Lafeu's daughter are going forward in the King's presence. But when Diana enters with her accusations, we have a situation roughly paralleling his earlier rejection of Helena. He scornfully repels her charges:

> My lord, this is a fond and desp'rate creature,
> Whom sometime I have laughed with. Let your Highness
> Lay a more noble thought upon mine honour
> Than for to think that I would sink it here.

Confronted with the evidence of the ring which had been the King's gift to Helena and his own ring which Diana produces to warrant her charges, he resorts to one lie after another, while his shifts grow more anguished and transparent, until the King at last exclaims:

> You boggle shrewdly, every feather starts you.

Parolles, who has returned to Roussillon, is called to testify but characteristically only adds further words to the confusion. Diana, who has been ordered to prison by the King in his irritation and suspicion of all concerned, is now brought back. But she adds further riddles, until, at the moment of utmost suspense, she produces Helena.

All of this may seem needlessly indirect to a reader, especially if he anticipates the solution; but in the theater it will create the necessary sense of growing pressure upon Bertram, of his assurance gradually undermined, until his pride is ready to break under the shock of the apparently miraculous reappearance of Helena.

The whole thing has been obviously contrived; but we have been allowed to see enough of the contrivance, in Helena's earlier prediction:

> You, Diana,
> Under my poor instruction yet must suffer
> Something in my behalf;

and in our knowledge that Diana's petition really comes from Helena, to realize that

Diana is acting on Helena's behalf. This is all the warrant we need for her conduct, and we can see its effect upon Bertram. But that Helena herself should bring this pressure directly to bear upon Bertram would be out of the question. Diana is a perfect substitute. She gains sanction for her boldness from our partiality for Helena, without prejudicing Helena's modesty; for we never identify the two.

When Helena herself enters, the King exclaims wonderingly,

> Is there no exorcist
> Beguiles the truer office of mine eyes?
> Is't real that I see?

And Helena's reply has no suggestion of triumph but only the memory of her former pathos:

> No, my good lord;
> 'Tis but the shadow of a wife you see,
> The name and not the thing.

As Bertram exclaims brokenly,

> Both, both. O, pardon!

it is to him she turns to make her appeal, not to the King:

> Will you be mine, now you are doubly won?

The happiness of the occasion is marked by Lafeu. His poor shadow of a daughter Maudlin, who never appeared on the stage, is forgotten. He claps Parolles on the back, borrows his handkerchief, and invites him to "make sport" with him at home. Even the basest character, once he has repented or been humbled, can be forgiven in Shakespeare. His lowly example generalizes our attitude to the hero. If Lafeu can accept Parolles, we should be able to accept Bertram. There is no need, of course, to represent Helena's forgiveness of Bertram; she has nothing to forgive. She is not that kind of character.

Critics have remarked, since Dr. Johnson's time, upon the abruptness of the play's ending. But everything depends upon the plausibility of Bertram's repentance and our final impression of Helena. If Bertram's repentance has carried emotional conviction for us, a dwelling upon his past faults can only raise a doubt of the permanence of his reformation. And certainly, the less said about the means by which Helena has brought events to a happy issue at the end, the better. She is not meant to appear as the clever contriver of her own success.

If the foregoing analysis affords a just view of the effect aimed at in the stage presentation of *All's Well*, it is clear that the chief concern of the play is with the study of character. *All's Well* is Helena's story, as Boccaccio's is the story of Giletta of Narbonne; but whereas Giletta is simply a folklore heroine whose cleverness wins her a husband, Shakespeare's Helena is a serious study of the virtue of humility in love. The effort is to maintain this impression of Helena consistently throughout the action and at the same time to prepare for Bertram's repentance and the reconciliation with Helena that follows; and the controlling idea of the play that emerges is the conception of Helena's love as far stronger than Bertram's arrogance, a love which works unobtrusively and with humility toward an end that heaven favors and thus issues in happiness.

But the idea is never obtruded upon us in a moral, as in simpler pieces like *How A Man May Choose A Good Wife From A Bad* or George Wilkins' *Miseries Of Enforced Marriage*, which are more aptly described as "problem plays" than *All's Well*, because they do deal unmistakably with social or ethical problems and comment upon them overtly. Shakespeare is never obviously didactic. His ideas are so fully transmuted into the dramatic terms of characters acting that we may argue endlessly about the motives of a Helena or a Bertram and imagine their lives beyond the confines of the play itself, as if they were people we might have known. As we read *All's Well* and consider the discrepancies between Helena's actions in the latter part of the play and her professed purposes, we may reflect that she is something of a sly minx, after all, just as we sometimes suspect ulterior motives in our own acquaintance. It seems clear enough, however, that Shakespeare has taken pains to avoid giving this impression of her in the theater, and that Shakespeare's audience would not think of her in this way.

The argument of this paper assumes that the dramatist tries to create an illusion of verisimilitude, that the play is an imitation of life, at least one remove from actuality. The play is intended for continuous performance before an audience that has not meditated upon the text and that will most readily follow the interpretive emphasis the dramatist has given the characters in the action that unfolds upon the stage. In reading *All's Well* we may readily forget this, because we can perceive the play's weakness clearly enough upon reflection. The temptation is to make our criticism a catalogue of errors—Shakespeare's, the Elizabethan audience's, or the ubiquitous collaborator's. The poetry has few splendid passages, compared with Shakespeare's best work; also

the text of the First Folio—the only authority for this play—is quite faulty. But the artifice that the critical reader detects in the construction and characterization may prove the saving grace of the play in performance; and it may be conjectured— lacking the evidence of a stage performance, which has seldom been ventured for *All's Well* within recent times [12]—that the play is contrived with sufficient skill to render Helena consistently appealing and her reconciliation with Bertram plausible and moving even for a modern audience unbiased by too close a knowledge of the strictures of the commentators.

[12] Within the present century, the play has been twice presented at Stratford (1916, 1922), at the Old Vic (1921), and by the Elizabethan Stage Society under the direction of William Poel (1920). In the United States, the play was performed at the Pasadena Playhouse under the supervision of Mr. Gilmor Brown and directed by Mr. Maxwell Sholes, November 26–27, 1937. For records of earlier performances, see the essay on the stage-history of the play by Harold Child in the Cambridge ed., pp. 187–89; Hazelton Spencer, *The Art and Life of William Shakespeare* (1940), p. 295.

Clifford Leech

The Theme of Ambition in *All's Well that Ends Well* [1]

AMONG critics of recent years who have offered us interpretations of *Troilus and Cressida*, *All's Well* and *Measure for Measure*, there has been a tendency to drop the expression "dark comedies" and to replace it by "problem comedies" or "problem plays." This, of course, is because we are now shy of seeing these plays as evidence that their writer suffered from an unusual depression of spirit during their period of composition. But even the term "problem comedies" is often applied to them in a very restricted sense. The problem exists, we are told, not for Shakespeare but for us. If we can get into a sufficiently Elizabethan frame of mind, we shall see that these plays are as orthodox in their thought and feeling as, say, *Gorboduc* or *The Honest Whore*. *Troilus and Cressida*, if we are to believe Professor T. W. Baldwin,[2] is only the first part of a straightforward dramatic chronicle of the Trojan War; *All's Well* is puzzling, according to Professor W. W. Lawrence,[3] only because we find it difficult to credit the ready Elizabethan acceptance of folk-tale plotting: its simple message, according to Miss M. C. Bradbrook,[4] is that "Virtue is

the true nobility"; *Measure for Measure*, we are told by many commentators (Professor Ernst Theodor Sehrt[5] being the latest but perhaps the most cautious among them), is an exposition of the idea of Christian mercy. All these critics would doubtless agree that *All's Well* and *Measure for Measure* are not so successfully put together as the major tragedies and the more popular comedies. In the "problem plays," says Dr. Tillyard,[6] Shakespeare was concerned "with either religious dogma or abstract speculation or both," and this concern was not fully absorbed into the structure of the plays, as it was in the major tragedies. The action of *All's Well* or of *Measure for Measure* is not a highly suitable medium for the exposition of the governing idea of the play. And in *All's Well* the verse has often a strange frigidity, as if the poet's mind was labouring.

There are, of course, considerable differences between any two of the three plays in question. In many ways it is unfortunate that *Troilus and Cressida* should commonly be associated with the others: its problems are vaster, its achievement not to be questioned in the same way as theirs. And though Shakespeare must have had *All's Well* very much in mind as he wrote *Measure for Measure*, the later play is a more disturbing problem because it so evidently contains better work. But the three plays are alike in that at different moments with-

[1] This paper was read on 17 August 1953 to the Sixth Shakespeare Conference held at the Shakespeare Institute, Stratford-upon-Avon.

[2] "Structural Analysis of 'Troilus and Cressida'" (*Shakespeare-Studien: Festschrift für Heinrich Mutschmann*, Marburg, 1951, pp. 5–18). A condensed version of this article is included in the New Variorum *Troilus and Cressida*, Philadelphia and London, 1953, pp. 450–4.

[3] *Shakespeare's Problem Comedies*, New York, 1931, p. 38.

[4] "Virtue is the True Nobility. A Study of the Structure of *All's Well that Ends Well*" (*Review of English Studies*, n.s. i (October 1950), 289–301). Miss Bradbrook has summarised this article

in her *Shakespeare and Elizabethan Poetry*, London, 1951, pp. 162–70.

[5] *Vergebung und Gnade bei Shakespeare*, Stuttgart, 1952, pp. 121–97.

[6] *Shakespeare's Problem Plays*, London, 1950, p. 3.

Reprinted from *ELH* (*A Journal of English Literary History*), XXI (March 1954), 17–29, by permission of the Johns Hopkins University Press.

in each attitudes are set up which are strangely at odds with one another. Hector tells us with authority that " 'Tis mad idolatry To make the service greater than the god," yet his last act is to rob a coward Greek of his sumptuous armour; Ulysses asserts the need for re-establishing degree, yet uses the arguments of emulation when he is in Achilles' company; Troilus wins our sympathy as he desires and loses, yet we see him at the end using warfare as an outlet for frustrated lust, unknowingly eager, as Thersites puts it, to "tickle it for his concupy." But in *Troilus*, as in the great tragedies, these contradictory impressions of the characters seem fused. As we see the play, we are only half-aware of them, as we are of the contradictions in our own habitual thought and action. The vision of life is so intense in *Troilus* and in the tragedies, the characters have the full impress of humanity on them, the verse they speak has an authority that will not let us raise objections. The things said in *Troilus* or in *Othello* may puzzle us afterwards, when we have left the theatre or are turning back over the pages of the book, but we are not puzzled when the play is an immediate experience. But that is not true of *Measure for Measure* or of *All's Well*. We lack there the sense of fusion: the esemplastic power does not seem to have been fully at work: the separate acts and utterances of Isabella and the Duke and Helena and the King of France are "fixities and definites" which resist compounding.

One of these fixities and definites in *All's Well* is, I think, the element of ambition which is entwined with Helena's love for Bertram. This element has been recognised before: Miss Bradbrook[7] has called her "a social climber," and Dr. Tillyard[8] has bracketed her with Parolles as "the two adventurers," adding however the qualifying words "one good the other contemptible." But my impression is that this element in the play, though recognised, has never been sufficiently attended to and that,

in particular, its relation to other comments on ambition in the early seventeenth century has been overlooked. Before, however, considering how this theme is handled in the play, it will be well to remind ourselves of a number of the other elements which go to make up *All's Well:* some of them are uneasy companions with one another, but some provide a useful setting for a dramatic comment on ambition.

We can, first of all, recognise with Professor Lawrence a strong element of folk-tale romance. Here, indeed, are the Healing of the King and the Fulfilling of the Tasks. We are meant to respond to these things as we respond to the casket-story in *The Merchant of Venice,* to the solving of Antiochus' riddle in *Pericles*. But though Shakespeare, in using such stories, meant his audience to respond in that simple way, we may note that the atmosphere and the characterisation in the France of *All's Well* are different from those of Belmont and Antioch. Quiller-Couch[9] rightly pointed out that we have a much less firm sense of the background of action in *All's Well* than in *Measure for Measure,* yet the atmosphere suggested, if not fully realized, in the picture of the Countess's household and the King's court is a real-life atmosphere. This makes it more difficult to enter readily into the story of a half-magical cure or the story of apparent impossibilities brought to pass. Perhaps because Shakespeare felt something of this difficulty, he reinforced the folk-tale element by giving it a Christian colouring: Helena in her curing of the King is a dispenser of divine grace, and in her definitive subjection of Bertram she is setting his foot on the path of Christian virtue. Dr. Tillyard[10] has observed that the use of formal verse in her scene with the King confers a ritual quality on the drama similar to that given by the Duke's rhymed octosyllabics in *Measure for Measure*. Yet here, in this deliberately exalted writing, we find it

---

[7] *Op. cit.,* p. 297.   [8] *Op. cit.,* p. 106.

[9] *All's Well that Ends Well* (New Cambridge edition), Cambridge, 1929, p. xxxiv.
[10] *Op. cit.,* pp. 100–2, 151–4.

odd that the minister of grace should speak
at times with the accent of the Player-
Queen: perhaps Shakespeare, not working
at full pressure on the play, relaxed too
much when he wrote these couplets, or perhaps his more critical feelings about Helena
enter almost surreptitiously even into this
scene. We may, indeed, note a similar phenomenon in I. i, when the Countess gives
parting advice to her son, using the sentiments and the idiom of Polonius. Even so,
the folk-tale stories and the Christian colouring are strangely companioned by the
other elements that we should now turn to.

The play shows us old and young characters juxtaposed, with the old rebuking
the young and sighing at the present corruption of manners. On the one side the
King, the Countess, Lafeu, the dead fathers
of Bertram and Helena; on the other Bertram and Parolles. In I. i the Countess has
no illusions about her son, and hopes for
his amendment at court; in I. ii the King
holds forth on the virtues of the dead
Count, and on the imperfections of young
courtiers of later days. Bertram's father,
he says, was fortunate in dying before he
could see the new generation raise its head
in full obnoxiousness. He ends his speech
with an echo of the dying Henry IV, who
had also found cause to look alarmed on
the young. This element, which links *All's
Well* with the most thoughtful of Shakespeare's histories, takes us far away from
the atmosphere of a folk-tale. It suggests,
we may say, a "darkening" of the view. But
it would be wrong to see the old in this
play as models of conduct, against which
the shortcomings of the young are measured. There is here a critical element with
a scope wide enough to touch all the characters presented. We have seen strange notes
brought into the language of Helena and
the Countess, and there are other utterances
in the play which take us continually by
surprise. In II. i Bertram has been told that
he is "Too young" to go to the war: the
King, bidding other lords farewell, labori-
ously jests:

> Those girls of Italy, take heed of them;
> They say our French lack language to deny,
> If they demand; beware of being captives
> Before you serve.

Soon Bertram, before serving, is to face
such a demand, and will be strongly rebuked for finding "language to deny." The
King's joke should perhaps not be taken
too seriously, but it is odd to find it where
it is. In the following scene we leave the
court for Rousillon, and there find the
Clown mocking at court manners: it is,
says Professor Dover Wilson,[11] "silly stuff,"
and no one will disagree, yet it has a
strange impact in immediately following
our first view of the French court. The matter of the Florentine war is cursorily handled in the play, yet has on occasion a certain interest. In I. ii the French King de-
cides not to support Florence, because
Austria, "our dearest friend," will not
have it so. In III. i the Duke of Florence
has addressed the French lords on the justice of his cause: the lords are convinced,
and the Second Lord confesses himself
baffled by his King's decision. But the
young lords are not primarily interested
in the goodness of the cause: they come to
Florence "For breathing and exploit," "for
physic" after surfeiting on their ease. We
are made to look forward to a later handling of this theme, when the Volscian serv-
ants in *Coriolanus* rejoiced that they would
"have a stirring world again." Perhaps, too,
we can find a touch of acid in the Duke of
Florence's promise of advancement to the
French lords:

> You know your places well;
> When better fall, for your avails they fell.

This we should bear in mind when we find
Bertram doing so well in his military ca-
reer. Partly Shakespeare may have emphasised his success in order to make him fit
better into the folk-tale setting: Helena's
prize, in that context of thought, should be

11 *All's Well that Ends Well* (New Cambridge
edition), p. 143.

worth having. But it may be significant too that he was excelling in a field where high politics were murky, where promotion depended on casualties on one's own side, and where Ajax and Achilles had recently been men of note. But this satirical element in *All's Well* shows itself too in the complications of the ending. The dénouement is not so skilfully managed as in *Measure for Measure*, where Shakespeare seems to have had his mind set alight by the very ingenuity of his own plotting. In the earlier play the devices seem clumsily fetched in. We are told in IV. v that Bertram had once been intended to marry Lafeu's daughter, as if Shakespeare had just thought of this. So we learn for the first time that Helena's ring, which she put on Bertram's finger in the night, was originally given her by the King. And the King, unlike the Duke in *Measure for Measure*, is in this scene as baffled as anyone: he is ready to believe any accusation made, any suspicion that comes to sudden birth in his mind. He is driven to a somewhat absurd impatience with Diana, and cries out at length: "Take her away. I do not like her now." Yet at the end he is promising to give her any husband of her choosing. He had not, it appears, come to realise the trouble that such a practice could lead to. In this last scene there is, too, a curious broadness of speech in Diana. To the King she says: "By Jove, if ever I knew man, 'twas you." A moment later she indicates Lafeu and says: "I am either maid, or else this old man's wife." If these assertions are meant only to amuse, they are not amusing enough. The Helena-Bertram story needed a formal scene of recognition and repentance, and a King was available among the dramatis personae to preside over the affair. But, like Chapman in *The Widow's Tears* and Jonson in *Volpone*, Shakespeare did not here remain wholly content with the court of justice that he had set up. His criticism is not so conscious a thing as Chapman's or Jonson's: partly he is genuinely concerned to arrive at a good ending

for the play, but there seems an undercurrent of rebelliousness which makes the judge appear ridiculous and the chief witness impertinent. Shakespeare makes Bertram repent, accept the King's mercy and Helena's discipline, but the matter is perfunctorily handled. We are reminded of the repentance of Proteus in *The Two Gentlemen* when Bertram gives us his last words:

> If she, my liege, can make me know this clearly,
> I'll love her dearly, ever, ever dearly.

We leave him with no affection, no conviction. Yet Parolles, whose pretences had been exposed earlier, grows in the last part of the play: he is allowed, after his unmasking, to speak in soliloquy, and we recognize a certain humanity in him. "Simply the thing I am Shall make me live": that shows a readiness to live in the mud of contempt, but also an awareness of his own nature that Bertram never reaches. Parolles will never be worthy of respect, but he has learned the hardest lesson. He becomes almost a measure for the continuing pretences and self-trust of the rest of the play's characters.

Together with all this, we have the presentation of a young woman in love, resolute to gain her husband and to bring him to heel. That she is genuinely in love with Bertram we can have no doubt. In I. i she weeps at his going, and sees him as "a bright particular star"; in I. iii the Countess's Steward reports her as speaking "in the most bitter touch of sorrow that e'er I heard virgin exclaim in," and later in the play there is no question of her desolation when Bertram rudely deserts her. Nor should we be surprised that the object of her love is so unsatisfactory: before this time Julia had loved Proteus, Hero Claudio. In contemplating this new love-story, Shakespeare was perhaps more fully aware of the irrationality of the passion. But this play does not merely show us a good woman's love for an indifferent man: we are made to think analytically of the woman too. First there is Helena's pretence that she is weeping for her father when her tears are truly caused by Bertram's leaving Rousillon for Paris: we are early prepared for her skill in deception. Then she engages in talk with Parolles concerning virginity. Parolles asks her: "Are you meditating on virginity?" That enquiry could easily be turned aside: it is Helena who pursues the matter until it becomes a debate. When she asks "How might one do, sir, to lose it to her own liking?", it is evident that she would not keep it long if she could lose it in the way that pleased her. Parolles is not much interested in her liking, but his reply —"Marry, ill to like him that ne'er it likes" —might have dissuaded from her path a woman less determined. From this dialogue we can understand why Helena was ill content to be a virgin wife. She does indeed risk much to win her aim. She has to endure Bertram's first refusal, his desertion, his danger in the war, his mother's loss of him, his infidelity. All ends well, but before that the house at Rousillon knew much trouble. In I. iii the Clown associates her with Helen of Troy, which in this context is no great compliment. His song seems to equate the Countess with Hecuba, lamenting the wreck that Helen has brought. We may remind ourselves that the name Helen or Helena is Shakespeare's choice for the woman of this story, and that it is Paris that she goes to for her husband. This is not the only reminiscence of *Troilus and Cressida* that we can find in the play. In II. i when Lafeu brings Helena to the King, he speaks of her first as one who through her beauty alone can put life into the old:

> I have seen a medicine
> That's able to breathe life into a stone,
> Quicken a rock, and make you dance canary
> With spritely fire and motion; whose simple touch
> Is powerful to araise King Pepin, nay,
> To give great Charlemain a pen in's hand
> And write to her a love-line.

This emphasis on Helena's sexual attractiveness is given an extra twist when Lafeu leaves Helena with the King: "I am Cressid's uncle, That dare leave two together." The scene that follows shows us Helena claiming her father's skill, and promising heavenly benefits, yet we cannot forget, after Lafeu's words, what she has in truth come about. Lafeu will bring her to the King, who will bring her to Bertram, as Pandarus brought Cressida to Troilus. And she resembles Cressida too in a certain obliquity of utterance. At the end of the first scene in the play, she announces in soliloquy that the King's illness may give her a chance of winning Bertram. Yet in I. iii when the Countess compels her to admit her love, she protests that she knows it hopeless:

> My friends were poor, but honest; so's my love.
> Be not offended, for it hurts not him
> That he is lov'd of me; I follow him not
> By any token of presumptuous suit,
> Nor would I have him till I do deserve him;
> Yet never know how that desert should be.
> I know I love in vain, strive against hope;

The Countess is not so easily deceived. She would welcome Helena as a daughter-in-law, but she knows there is more information to extract:

> Had you lately an intent—speak truly—
> To go to Paris?

Then Helena admits that she plans to cure the King and, on further cross-questioning, that it was Bertram's presence in Paris that made her think of this. Beyond that she does not go, and the Countess does not press her. There is deception too in her use of the bed-trick, and something is still to be said on the impression that it makes on us and perhaps made on the Elizabethans. The situation is not so complicated as it was to be in *Measure for Measure,* for here we are not concerned with cohabitation without the blessing of the church. But it is a deception, and our attitude to a deception depends on the context, the atmosphere within which it is practised. In relation to the folk-tale element, Shakespeare wanted us to accept it as a legitimate device, and for this reason its lawfulness is emphasised in III. vii. But the atmosphere of the play as a whole is neither that of folk-tale nor that of brisk comedy. Miss Bradbrook [12] has wisely said of Giletta and Beltramo, the characters in Boccaccio corresponding to Helena and Bertram: "These shrewd, unsentimental, vigorous Italians, who come to terms after a brisk skirmish, resemble Beatrice and Benedick rather than their own Shakespearian descendants." And though perhaps we could not easily accept the bed-trick as part of the love-story of Beatrice and Benedick, it would certainly not be out of place in the good-humoured atmosphere of, say, *The Two Angry Women of Abington*. I recently came upon it, used most agreeably and comically, in a Lope de Vega farce. Professor H. S. Wilson [13] has said that "If we object to the play because of the 'bed-trick,' we reject the story itself, regardless of the execution." But this is to assume that in every situation our canons of judgment are identical—which is manifestly false. Thus, Dr. Tillyard [14] has observed that in *Measure for Measure* the context is too serious for us to accept the device, but he claims that there is not sufficient moral earnestness in *All's Well* for the same feeling of repugnance to arise. Here, I think, he depends too much on Professor Lawrence's emphasis on the folk-tale element in the play. We have seen that there is a good deal of acid in the play's thought, and it should be evident that the characters belong closely to our world. In such circumstances the device can hardly bring comfort. We could still accept it as an amusing piece of unscrupulousness, as we might, for example, if Ann Whitefield secured John Tanner that way, but the words of Helena are too full of high sentence for us to be amused by her obliquity. It may be worth noting that in Middleton's *The Witch* Isabella is contracted to Sebastian but, believing him dead, marries Antonio. Before the marriage is consummated, Sebastian returns from abroad and plans to enjoy Isabella by impersonating Antonio. He believes, in fact, like any good Elizabethan scholar, that Isabella is truly his wife. Yet when it comes to the point of action, he has scruples which never occurred to Mariana or Helena. Indeed the Elizabethans would see the bed-trick as a perhaps clever, perhaps amusing, perhaps unscrupulous form of deception. As such, it could never be a convenient instrument for the wholly admirable character.

Thus the love of Helena is not presented in an altogether sympathetic way, and that should not surprise us. Professor Lawrence Babb [15] has shown how ambivalent was the Elizabethan attitude towards love. It was at once the fine feeling of courtly lovers and a sickness that needed cure. Either of these attitudes might be dominant at different times and in different plays, but in serious plays where love was the dramatist's prominent concern, it was likely that the two attitudes should exist together, should form yet another of those contradictions especially characteristic of the Elizabethan mind. Though Shakespeare's gaze is shifting in *All's Well*, so that he appears to see the action and the characters differently at different moments, his scrutiny of Helena was at times searching. She was resolute and had a sense of virtue, she was praised by the old and reverend, she had at times a touch of modesty, she could feel pain. Yet she was going through a time of sickness, from which, as Countess of Rousillon, she would doubtless recover. This indeed is what the old Countess says when she looks at Helena in I. iii and thinks of the pangs of love:

Even so it was with me when I was young.
If ever we are nature's, these are ours; this thorn

---

[12] *Op. cit.*, p. 292.
[13] "Dramatic Emphasis in *All's Well that Ends Well*" (*Huntington Library Quarterly*, xiii (May 1950), 217–40).
[14] *Op. cit.*, p. 97.
[15] *The Elizabethan Malady*, East Lansing, 1951, p. 154.

Doth to our rose of youth rightly belong;
Our blood to us, this to our blood is born.
It is the show and seal of nature's truth,
Where love's strong passion is impress'd in
    youth.
By our remembrances of days foregone,
Such were our faults, or then we thought them
    none.
Her eye is sick on't;

Love is a "thorn," its manifestations are
"faults," the eye of the sufferer is "sick."
With Helena we are a long way from the
simply-fancied devotion of Julia and Hero.

But she is not merely sick, she is determined on her cure. And that is the loss of
her virginity, the subduing of Bertram to
her will. Here at last we turn to that element in the play which it is my main purpose to underline. I am not suggesting that
this gives us the key to the play, but that
the dramatist's attitude is made plainer if
we bear this in mind, and see ambition as
the force that turns Helena from a passive
lovesickness to active planning. In her first
soliloquy she speaks of "Th' ambition in
my love," and at the end of the first scene,
again in soliloquy, her belief in her own
power is akin to that of any ambitious hero
of the time:

Our remedies oft in ourselves do lie,
Which we ascribe to heaven. The fated sky
Gives us free scope; only doth backward pull
Our slow designs when we ourselves are
    dull. . . .
Impossible be strange attempts to those
That weigh their pains in sense, and do suppose
What hath been cannot be.

We must remember that this is the period
of Chapman's Bussy, Jonson's Sejanus,
Shakespeare's Edmund. They believe alike
in their own power, and each dramatist has
taken pains to make us see the vanity of the
things they work for. Here the satiric element in All's Well is important, for we are
made to see the value of Helena's prize: she
becomes the wife of Bertram, a good fighter
and a liar, cowed by the King, deceived by
Parolles, by Diana and by Helena herself;

she becomes Countess of Rousillon, a mem-
ber of a chap-fallen nobility. And, as so
often with the ambitious man or woman,
there is something of ostentation in her.
Robert Ashley in his treatise Of Honour,
probably written shortly before All's Well,
urged that we should avoid ostentation in
our manner as ambition in our minds. It
was better, he said, to incline towards the
other extreme:

Whiles we endevour therfore after true honour, all
kind of ostentacion ys to be eschewed, and we
ought rather to decline to th'other extreame of too
much deieccion, that by how much the farther we
depart from the vice, we may meet so much the
sooner with the meane: especially since the mind
of man being by nature puffed vp, ys rather to be
somewhat abased then to be lyfted high, least yt
become intollerable and insolent: [16]

Perhaps that is why Helena, in claiming
efficacy for the remedy she brought, spoke
to the King in the language of the Player-
Queen. And there is something "intollerable
and insolent" in her elaborate planning of
the final victory, though it is true that her
words remain modest. In Boccaccio and
Paynter, Giletta and Beltramo meet as it
were on equal terms: there is no King to
threaten Beltramo with death, no Countess
or Lafeu to look disapprovingly on the
young man, no false witness to bring all
momentarily to confusion. Giletta has performed the tasks, announces the fact, and
demands her reward. Beltramo can take it
in good part. But Helena prepares busily
indeed for the dénouement. In IV. iii we
learn that false news of Helena's death has
been brought to Bertram. In the next scene
Helena tells Diana and the Widow: "You
must know I am supposed dead." We must
assume therefore that the lie is hers, that
her object is to bring Bertram to bewilder-
ment and fear. There follows her use of
Diana as a false witness, and a witness who
proceeds to contradict herself. Only when
her devices are exhausted does she come to
rescue Bertram and take him in her charge.

[16] Of Honour, edited by Virgil B. Heltzel, San
Marino, 1947, p. 57.

If she had married the Duke of Vienna, the season of masquerade might have lasted the whole year long.

The effect of the play as we have it is blurred, and the closely related things that I have stressed—the satiric presentation of the background, the nature of Helena's love and her ambition—do not emerge clearly in the total effect and are often barely noticeable in the individual scenes. Yet there is, I think, something of "darkness" here, and there is at least an aesthetic problem—the problem of the dramatist's failure in imagination. A traditional story and realistic characterisation can be fused, as in *Lear*. So, too, we feel no unease when a Christian colouring is present along with a sharply critical view of the world, as I think in *Macbeth*. But here there is no fusion. We must recognize the possibility of revision and collaboration, and certainly the text has been ill-treated. But we should not be too much surprised that sometimes the magic would not work, that Shakespeare could give us a play as confused in effect as, say, *The Devil's Law-Case*.

A. W. Schlegel

Measure for Measure

IN *Measure for Measure* Shakspeare was compelled, by the nature of the subject, to make his poetry more familiar with criminal justice than is usual with him. All kinds of proceedings connected with the subject, all sorts of active or passive persons, pass in review before us: the hypocritical Lord Deputy, the compassionate Provost, and the hard-hearted Hangman; a young man of quality who is to suffer for the seduction of his mistress before marriage, loose wretches brought in by the police, nay, even a hardened criminal, whom even the preparations for his execution cannot awaken out of his callousness. But yet, notwithstanding this agitating truthfulness, how tender and mild is the pervading tone of the picture! The piece takes improperly its name from punishment; the true significance of the whole is the triumph of mercy over strict justice; no man being himself so free from errors as to be entitled to deal it out to his equals. The most beautiful embellishment of the composition is the character of Isabella, who, on the point of taking the veil, is yet prevailed upon by sisterly affection to tread again the perplexing ways of the world, while, amid the general corruption, the heavenly purity of her mind is not even stained with one unholy thought: in the humble robes of the novice she is a very angel of light. When the cold and stern Angelo, heretofore of unblemished reputation, whom the Duke has commissioned, during his pretended absence, to restrain, by a rigid administration of the laws, the excesses of dissolute immorality, is even himself tempted by the virgin charms of Isabella, supplicating for the pardon of her brother Claudio, condemned to death for a youthful indiscretion; when at first, in timid and obscure language, he insinuates, but at last impudently avouches his readiness to grant Claudio's life to the sacrifice of her honour; when Isabella repulses his offer with a noble scorn; in her account of the interview to her brother, when the latter at first applauds her conduct, but at length, overcome by the fear of death, strives to persuade her to consent to dishonour;—in these masterly scenes, Shakspeare has sounded the depths of the human heart. The interest here reposes altogether on the represented action; curiosity contributes nothing to our delight, for the Duke, in the disguise of a Monk, is always present to watch over his dangerous representative, and to avert every evil which could possibly be apprehended; we look to him with confidence for a happy result. The Duke acts the part of the Monk naturally, even to deception; he unites in his person the wisdom of the priest and the prince. Only in his wisdom he is too fond of round-about ways; his vanity is flattered with acting invisibly like an earthly providence; he takes more pleasure in overhearing his subjects than governing them in the customary way of princes. As he ultimately extends a free pardon to all the guilty, we do not see how his original purpose, in committing the execution of the laws to other hands, of restoring their strictness, has in any wise been accomplished. The poet might have had this irony in view, that of the numberless slanders of the Duke, told him by the petulant Lucio, in ignorance of the person whom he is addressing, that at least which regarded his

Reprinted from *A Course of Lectures on Dramatic Art and Literature*, trans. John Black (London: Henry G. Bohn, 1846), pp. 387–88. First German edition, 1809.

singularities and whims was not wholly without foundation. It is deserving of remark, that Shakspeare, amidst the rancour of religious parties, takes a delight in painting the condition of a monk, and always represents his influence as beneficial. We find in him none of the black and knavish monks, which an enthusiasm for Protestantism, rather than poetical inspiration, has suggested to some of our modern poets. Shakspeare merely gives his monks an inclination to busy themselves in the affairs of others, after renouncing the world for themselves; with respect, however, to pious frauds, he does not represent them as very conscientious. Such are the parts acted by the monk in *Romeo and Juliet,* and another in *Much Ado About Nothing,* and even by the Duke, whom, contrary to the well-known proverb, the cowl seems really to make a monk.

Walter Pater

Measure for Measure

. . . Of Angelo we may feel at first sight inclined to say only *guarda e passa!* or to ask whether he is indeed psychologically possible. In the old story, he figures as an embodiment of pure and unmodified evil, like "Hyliogabalus of Rome or Denis of Sicyll." But the embodiment of pure evil is no proper subject of art, and Shakespeare, in the spirit of a philosophy which dwells much on the complications of outward circumstance with men's inclinations, turns into a subtle study in casuistry this incident of the austere judge fallen suddenly into utmost corruption by a momentary contact with supreme purity. But the main interest in *Measure for Measure* is not, as in *Promos and Cassandra*, in the relation of Isabella and Angelo, but rather in the relation of Claudio and Isabella.

Greek tragedy in some of its noblest products has taken for its theme the love of a sister, a sentiment unimpassioned indeed, purifying by the very spectacle of its passionlessness, but capable of a fierce and almost animal strength if informed for a moment by pity and regret. At first Isabella comes upon the scene as a tranquillising influence in it. But Shakespeare, in the development of the action, brings quite different and unexpected qualities out of her. It is his characteristic poetry to expose this cold, chastened personality, respected even by the worldly Lucio as "something ensky'd and sainted, and almost an immortal spirit," to two sharp, shameful trials, and wring out of her a fiery, revealing eloquence. Thrown into the terrible dilemma of the piece, called upon to sacrifice that cloistral whiteness to sisterly affection, be-come in a moment the ground of strong, contending passions, she develops a new character and shows herself suddenly of kindred with those strangely conceived women, like Webster's Vittoria, who unite to a seductive sweetness something of a dangerous and tigerlike changefulness of feeling. The swift, vindictive anger leaps, like a white flame, into this white spirit, and, stripped in a moment of all convention, she stands before us clear, detached, columnar, among the tender frailties of the piece. Cassandra, the original of Isabella in Whetstone's tale, with the purpose of the Roman Lucretia in her mind, yields gracefully enough to the conditions of her brother's safety; and to the lighter reader of Shakespeare there may seem something harshly conceived, or psychologically impossible even, in the suddenness of the change wrought in her, as Claudio welcomes for a moment the chance of life through her compliance with Angelo's will, and he may have a sense here of flagging skill, as in words less finely handled than in the preceding scene. The play, though still not without traces of nobler handiwork, sinks down, as we know, at last into almost homely comedy, and it might be supposed that just here the grander manner deserted it. But the skill with which Isabella plays upon Claudio's well-recognised sense of honour, and endeavours by means of that to insure him beforehand from the acceptance of life on baser terms, indicates no coming laxity of hand just in this place. It was rather that there rose in Shakespeare's conception, as there may for the reader, as there certainly would in any good acting of

Reprinted from *Appreciations* (London: Macmillan & Co., 1910), pp. 177–84. The essay, here excerpted, was first published in 1874.

the part, something of that terror, the seeking for which is one of the notes of romanticism in Shakespeare and his circle. The stream of ardent natural affection, poured as sudden hatred upon the youth condemned to die, adds an additional note of expression to the horror of the prison where so much of the scene takes place. It is not here only that Shakespeare has conceived of such extreme anger and pity as putting a sort of genius into simple women, so that their "lips drop eloquence," and their intuitions interpret that which is often too hard or fine for manlier reason; and it is Isabella with her grand imaginative diction, and that poetry laid upon the "prone and speechless dialect" there is in mere youth itself, who gives utterance to the equity, the finer judgments of the piece on men and things.

From behind this group with its subtle lights and shades, its poetry, its impressive contrasts, Shakespeare, as I said, conveys to us a strong sense of the tyranny of nature and circumstance over human action. The most powerful expressions of this side of experience might be found here. The bloodless, impassible temperament does but wait for its opportunity, for the almost accidental coherence of time with place, and place with wishing, to annul its long and patient discipline, and become in a moment the very opposite of that which under ordinary conditions it seemed to be, even to itself. The mere resolute self-assertion of the blood brings to others special temptations, temptations which, as defects or overgrowths, lie in the very qualities which make them otherwise imposing or attractive; the very advantage of men's gifts of intellect or sentiment being dependent on a balance in their use so delicate that men hardly maintain it always. Something also must be conceded to influences merely physical, to the complexion of the heavens, the skyey influences, shifting as the stars shift; as something also to the mere caprice of men exercised over each other in the dispensations of social or political order, to

the chance which makes the life or death of Claudio dependent on Angelo's will.

The many veins of thought which render the poetry of this play so weighty and impressive unite in the image of Claudio, a flowerlike young man, whom, prompted by a few hints from Shakespeare, the imagination easily clothes with all the bravery of youth, as he crosses the stage before us on his way to death, coming so hastily to the end of his pilgrimage. Set in the horrible blackness of the prison, with its various forms of unsightly death, this flower seems the braver. Fallen by "prompture of the blood," the victim of a suddenly revived law against the common fault of youth like his, he finds his life forfeited as if by the chance of a lottery. With that instinctive clinging to life, which breaks through the subtlest casuistries of monk or sage apologising for an early death, he welcomes for a moment the chance of life through his sister's shame, though he revolts hardly less from the notion of perpetual imprisonment so repulsive to the buoyant energy of youth. Familiarised, by the words alike of friends and the indifferent, to the thought of death, he becomes gentle and subdued indeed, yet more perhaps through pride than real resignation, and would go down to darkness at last hard and unblinded. Called upon suddenly to encounter his fate, looking with keen and resolute profile straight before him, he gives utterance to some of the central truths of human feeling, the sincere, concentrated expression of the recoiling flesh. Thoughts as profound and poetical as Hamlet's arise in him; and but for the accidental arrest of sentence he would descend into the dust, a mere gilded, idle flower of youth indeed, but with what are perhaps the most eloquent of all Shakespeare's words upon his lips.

As Shakespeare in *Measure for Measure* has refashioned, after a nobler pattern, materials already at hand, so that the relics of other men's poetry are incorporated into his perfect work, so traces of the old "morality," that early form of dramatic composi-

tion which had for its function the incul-
cating of some moral theme, survive in it
also, and give it a peculiar ethical interest.
This ethical interest, though it can escape
no attentive reader, yet, in accordance with
that artistic law which demands the pre-
dominance of form everywhere over the
mere matter or subject handled, is not to
be wholly separated from the special circumstances, necessities, embarrassments, of
these particular dramatic persons. The old
"moralities" exemplified most often some
rough-and-ready lesson. Here the very intricacy and subtlety of the moral world itself, the difficulty of seizing the true relations of so complex a material, the difficulty
of just judgment, of judgment that shall
not be unjust, are the lessons conveyed.
Even in Whetstone's old story this peculiar
vein of moralising comes to the surface:
even there, we notice the tendency to dwell
on mixed motives, the contending issues of
action, the presence of virtues and vices
alike in unexpected places, on "the hard
choice of two evils," on the "imprisoning"
of men's "real intents." *Measure for Measure* is full of expressions drawn from a profound experience of these casuistries, and
that ethical interest becomes predominant
in it: it is no longer *Promos and Cassandra,*
but *Measure for Measure,* its new name ex-
pressly suggesting the subject of *poetical
justice.* The action of the play, like the action of life itself for the keener observer,
develops in us the conception of this poetical justice, and the yearning to realise it,
the true justice of which Angelo knows
nothing, because it lies for the most part
beyond the limits of any acknowledged
law. The idea of justice involves the idea
of rights. But at bottom rights are equivalent to that which really is, to facts; and
the recognition of his rights therefore, the
justice he requires of our hands, or our
thoughts, is the recognition of that which
the person, in his inmost nature, really is;
and as sympathy alone can discover that
which really is in matters of feeling and
thought, true justice is in its essence a finer
knowledge through love.

'Tis very pregnant:
The jewel that we find we stoop and take it,
Because we see it; but what we do not see
We tread upon, and never think of it.

It is for this finer justice, a justice based
on a more delicate appreciation of the true
conditions of men and things, a true respect
of persons in our estimate of actions, that
the people in *Measure for Measure* cry out
as they pass before us; and as the poetry
of this play is full of the peculiarities of
Shakespeare's poetry, so in its ethics it is
an epitome of Shakespeare's moral judgments. They are the moral judgments of an
observer, of one who sits as a spectator,
and knows how the threads in the design
before him hold together under the surface:
they are the judgments of the humourist
also, who follows with a half-amused but
always pitiful sympathy, the various ways
of human disposition, and sees less distance
than ordinary men between what are called
respectively great and little things. It is
not always that poetry can be the exponent
of morality; but it is this aspect of morals
which it represents most naturally, for this
true justice is dependent on just those finer
appreciations which poetry cultivates in us
the power of making, those peculiar valu-
ations of action and its effect which poetry
actually requires.

Sir Walter Raleigh

Measure for Measure

IN criticisms of *Measure for Measure,* we are commonly presented with a picture of Vienna as a black pit of seething wickedness; and against this background there rises the dazzling, white, and saintly figure of Isabella. The picture makes a good enough Christmas card, but it is not Shakespeare. If the humorous scenes are needed only, as Professor Dowden says, "to present without disguise or extenuation a world of moral licence and corruption," why are they humorous? The wretches who inhabit the purlieus of the city are live men, pleasant to Shakespeare. Abhorson, the public executioner, is infamous by his profession, and is redeemed from infamy by his pride in it. When Pompey, who has followed a trade even lower in esteem, is offered to him as an assistant, his dignity rebels: "A bawd, Sir? Fie upon him, he will discredit our mystery." Pompey himself, the irrelevant, talkative clown, half a wit and half a dunce, is one of those humble, cheerful beings, willing to help in anything that is going forward, who are the mainstay of human affairs. Hundreds of them must do their daily work and keep their appointments, before there can be one great man of even moderate dimensions. Elbow, the thick-witted constable, own cousin to Dogberry, is no less dutiful. Froth is an amiable, feather-headed young gentleman—to dislike him would argue an ill nature, and a small one. Even Lucio has his uses; nor is it very plain that in his conversations with the Duke he forfeits Shakespeare's sympathy. He has a taste for scandal, but it is a mere luxury of idleness; though his tongue is loose, his heart is simply affectionate, and he is eager to help his friend.

Lastly, to omit none of the figures who make up the background, Mistress Overdone pays a strict attention to business, and is carried to prison in due course of law. This world of Vienna, as Shakespeare paints it, is not a black world; it is a weak world, full of little vanities and stupidities, regardful of custom, fond of pleasure, idle, and abundantly human. No one need go far to find it. On the other side, over against the populace, are ranged the officers of the government, who are more respectable, though hardly more amiable. The Duke, a man of the quickest intelligence and sympathy, shirks his public duties, and plays the benevolent spy. He cannot face the odious necessities of his position. The law must be enforced, and the man who enforces it, putting off all those softer human qualities which are dearest to him, must needs maim himself, for the good of the social machine. So the Duke, like many a head of a family or college, tries to keep the love of the rebels by putting his ugly duties upon the shoulders of a deputy, and goes into exile to watch the case secretly from the opposition side. Shakespeare does not condemn him, but permits him to learn from the careless talk of Lucio that he has gained no credit by his default of duty. In his place is installed the strong man, the darling and idol of weak governments. The Lord Deputy, Angelo, is given sole authority, and is prepared to put down lust and licence with a firm hand, making law absolute, and maintaining justice without exception. His defence of the strict application of law, as it is set forth in his speeches to his colleague, Escalus, contains some of the finest and truest things ever said on

Reprinted from *Shakespeare* (New York, 1907), pp. 165–73, by permission of Macmillan & Co. This selection is taken from Chapter 5, "Story and Character."

that topic. He has no misgivings, and offers a convincing proof of the need for severity.

So the train is laid. Quietly and naturally, out of ordinary human material, by the operation of the forces of every day, there is raised the mount on which Claudio and Isabella are to suffer their agony. A question of policy suddenly becomes a soul's tragedy. Claudio is in love with Juliet. Her friends are opposed to the match, and there has been no marriage ceremony: meantime, the lovers have met secretly, and Juliet is with child by him. The solution offered by Isabella is short and simple: "O, let him marry her." But the new and stricter reign of law has begun, old penalties have been revived, and Claudio must die. There is no appeal possible to the Duke, who has disappeared; and the one hope left is that Isabella may move the deputy to take pity on her brother. What she has to say is no answer to the reasons which have convinced Angelo that strict administration of the law is needful. The case contemplated has arisen, that is all. If, from tender consideration for the sinner, the law is to be defeated, will not the like considerations arise in every other case? It is worth remarking that Shakespeare hardly makes use of the best formal and casuistical arguments employed by Cinthio's heroine. After pleading the youth and inexperience of her brother, and discoursing on the power of love, the lady of the novel takes up the point of legality. The deputy, she says, is the living law; if his commands are merciful, they will still be legal. But the pleading of Isabella is for mercy as against the law. The logic of Angelo stands unshaken after her most eloquent assaults. He believes himself to be strong enough to do his duty; he has suppressed in himself all sensual pity, but sense is not to be denied; and it overcomes him by an unexpected attack from another quarter. The beauty and grace of Isabella, pleading the cause of guilty love, stir desire in him; and he propounds to her the disgraceful terms whereby Claudio's

life is to be saved at the expense of her honour. She does not, even in thought, entertain the proposal for an instant, but carries it to her brother in the prison, that her refusal may be reinforced by his. At the first blush, he joins in her indignant rejection of it. But when his imagination gets to work on the doom that is now certain, he pleads with her for his life. This is the last horror, and Isabella, in a storm of passion, withers Claudio by her contempt. "Let me ask my sister pardon," he says, when at last the Duke enters; "I am so out of love with life that I will sue to be rid of it." The rest of the play is mere plot, devised as a retreat, to save the name of Comedy.

Of all Shakespeare's plays, this one comes nearest to the direct treatment of a moral problem. What did he think of it all? He condemns no one, high or low. The meaning of the play is missed by those who forget that Claudio is not wicked, merely human, and fails only from sudden terror of the dark. Angelo himself is considerately and mildly treated; his hypocrisy is self-deception, not cold and calculated wickedness. Like many another man, he has a lofty, fanciful idea of himself, and his public acts belong to this imaginary person. At a crisis, the real man surprises the play-actor, and pushes him aside. Angelo had underestimated the possibilities of temptation:

> O cunning enemy, that to catch a saint
> With saints dost bait thy hook!

After the fashion of King Claudius in *Hamlet*, but with more sincerity, he tries to pray. It is useless; his old ideals for himself are a good thing grown tedious. While he is waiting for the interview with Isabella, the blood rushes to his heart, like a crowd round one who swoons, or a multitude pressing to the audience of a king. The same giddiness is felt by Bassanio in the presence of Portia, and is described by him in almost the same figures. When the wickedness of Angelo is unveiled, Isabella is willing to make allowances for him:

> I partly think
> A due sincerity governed his deeds,
> Till he did look on me.

But he is dismayed when he thinks of his fall, and asks for no allowance:

> So deep sticks it in my penitent heart,
> That I crave death more willingly than mercy;
> 'Tis my deserving, and I do entreat it.

Shakespeare, it is true, does not follow the novel by marrying him to Isabella, but he invents Mariana for him, and points him to happiness.

Is the meaning of the play centred in the part of Isabella? She is severe, and beautiful, and white with an absolute whiteness. Yet it seems that even she is touched now and again by Shakespeare's irony. She stands apart, and loses sympathy as an angel might lose it, by seeming to have too little stake in humanity:

> Then Isabel live chaste, and brother die;
> More than our brother is our chastity.

Perhaps it is the rhyming tag that gives to this a certain explicit and repulsive calmness: at the end of his scenes Shakespeare often makes his most cherished characters do the menial explanatory work of a chorus. He treats Cordelia no better, without the excuse, in this case, of a scene to be closed:

> For thee, oppressed king, I am cast down;
> Myself could else outfrown false Fortune's frown.

When we first make acquaintance with her, Isabella is on the eve of entering a cloister; we overhear her talking to one of the sisters, and expressing a wish that a more strict restraint were imposed upon the order. She is an ascetic by nature, and some of the Duke's remarks on the vanity of self-regarding virtue, though they are addressed to Angelo, seem to glance delicately at her. Shakespeare has left us in no doubt concerning his own views on asceticism; his poems and plays are full of eloquent passages directed against self-culture and the celibate ideal. In a wonderful line of *A Midsummer Night's Dream* he pictures the sisterhood of the cloister—

> Chanting faint hymns to the cold fruitless moon.

There is a large worldliness about him which makes him insist on the doctrine of usury. Virtue, he holds, is empty without beneficence:

> No man is the lord of anything,
> Till he communicate his parts to others.

He goes further, and, in a great passage of *Troilus and Cressida*, teaches how worth and merit may not dare to neglect or despise their reflection in the esteem of men. No man can know himself save as he is known to others. Honour is kept bright by perseverance in action: love is the price of love. It is not by accident that Shakespeare calls Isabella back from the threshold of the nunnery, and after passing her though the furnace of trial, marries her to the Duke. She too, like Angelo, is redeemed for worldly uses; and the seething city of Vienna had some at least of Shakespeare's sympathy as against both the true saint and the false.

In this play there is thus no single character through whose eyes we can see the questions at issue as Shakespeare saw them. His own thought is interwoven in every part of it; his care is to maintain the balance, and to show us every side. He stands between the gallants of the playhouse and the puritans of the city; speaking of charity and mercy to these; to those asserting the reality of virtue in the direst straits, when charity and mercy seem to be in league against it. Even virtue, answering to a sudden challenge, alarmed, and glowing with indignation, though it is a beautiful thing, is not the exponent of his ultimate judgment. His attitude is critical and ironical, expressed in reminders, and questions, and comparisons. When we seem to be committed to one party, he calls us back to a feeling of kinship with the other. He pleads for his creatures, as he pleads in the Sonnets for his friend:

> For to thy sensual fault I bring in sense;
> Thy adverse party is thy Advocate.

Measure for measure: the main theme of the play is echoed and re-echoed from speaker to speaker, and exhibited in many lights. "Plainly conceive, I love you," says Angelo; and quick as lightning comes Isabella's retort:

> My brother did love Juliet; and you tell me
> That he shall die for't.

The law is strict; but the offence that it condemns is knit up with humanity, so that in choosing a single victim the law seems unjust and tyrannical. Authority and degree, place and form, the very framework of human society, are subjected to the same irony:

> Respect to your great place; and let the devil
> Be sometime honour'd for his burning throne.

The thought that was painfully working in Shakespeare's mind reached its highest and fullest expression in the cry of King Lear:

> None does offend, none, I say none; I'll able 'em;
> Take that of me, my friend, who have the power
> To seal th' accuser's lips.

Many men make acquaintance with Christian morality as a branch of codified law, and dutifully adopt it as a guide to action, without the conviction and insight that are the fruit of experience. A few, like Shakespeare, discover it for themselves, as it was first discovered, by an anguish of thought and sympathy; so that their words are a revelation, and the gospel is born anew.

Sir Arthur Quiller-Couch

Measure for Measure

PATER says well:[1] and Shakespeare no doubt has the understanding, the capacity for this "finer justice." We have many another play for evidence; and in this one not a few flashes that show us the wrong-doer justifying himself to himself and under the law's frowning presence putting up an excuse to exist—as when Pompey pleads "Truly, sir, I am a poor fellow that would live."

Nevertheless an anthology of scattered passages and a solid play are two different things, and may produce a vastly different conviction: and Pater may accurately report what was working in Shakespeare's mind without convincing us that Shakespeare succeeded in expressing it: and if the total play does not clearly express this, then and to that extent it has failed, and the idea has not emerged, because in the author's mind it never attained to being thoroughly clear.

We submit that in *Measure for Measure*, as we have it, the idea is not thoroughly clear, has not been thoroughly realised. We take as our test Isabella; the "heroine" and mainspring of the whole action. Isabella, more than any other character in the play, should carry our sympathy with her, or, at the least, our understanding. But does she? On the contrary the critics can make nothing of her or—which is worse—they make two opposite women of her, and praise or blame her accordingly. We pass Lucio's obeisance—

I hold you as a thing enskied and sainted—

because sensualists like Lucio habitually divide women into two classes: the one comprising their animal prey, the other set apart as angels for the sentimental homage which vice pays to virtue. Shakespeare knew better than *that*. We take, rather, the opinions of two of her own sex upon this woman faced with the alternatives of sacrificing either her chastity or her brother's life, and upon the line of her decision. Mrs Jameson, in her *Characteristics of Women* (1832), drew a comparison, often quoted, between Isabella and the Portia of *The Merchant of Venice*. They are equally wise, gracious, fair and young; yet

Isabella is distinguished from Portia and strongly individualised by a certain moral grandeur, a saintly grace, something of vestal dignity and purity which render her less attractive and more imposing.

By Mrs Jameson's admission, then, she is less attractive than Portia: but Mrs Charlotte Lennox (still remembered as the Author of *The Female Quixote*), in her *Shakspear Illustrated*, published in 1753, can scarcely pardon Isabella at all, and indeed goes so far as to call her a "vixen," having her eye on the passage wherein she repels her brother—poor devil condemned to die—

>   O, you beast,
> O, faithless coward, O, dishonest wretch,
> Wilt thou be made a man out of my vice?
> Is't not a kind of incest, to take life
> From thine own sister's shame? What should I think?
> Heaven shield my mother played my father fair . . .
> For such a warpèd slip of wilderness

---

[1] The reference is to the discussion of poetic justice at the close of Pater's essay on *Measure for Measure*. See p. 68, above. [Ed.]

Reprinted from the New Cambridge edition of *Measure for Measure*, ed. A. Quiller-Couch & J. Dover Wilson (1922), pp. xxvii–xxxv, by permission of the Cambridge University Press. This selection consists of sections VIII, IX, and X of the Introduction.

Ne'er issued from his blood. . . . **Take my de-**
fiance,
Die, perish. . . . Might but my bending down
Reprieve thee from thy fate, it should pro-
ceed. . . .
I'll pray a thousand prayers for thy death,
No word to save thee.

Mrs Lennox comments:

From her character, her profession, and degree
of relation to the unhappy youth, one might have
expected mild expostulations, wise reasonings, and
gentle rebukes; his desire of life, though pur-
chased by methods he could not approve, was a
natural frailty which a sister might have pitied
and excused, and have made use of her superior
understanding to reason down his fears, recall
nobler ideas to his mind, teach him what was due
to her honour and his own, and reconcile him to
his approaching death by arguments drawn from
that religion and virtue of which she made so high
a profession: but that torrent of abusive language,
those coarse and unwomanly reflexions on the
virtue of her mother, her exulting cruelty to the
dying youth, are the manners of an affected prude,
outrageous in her seeming virtue; not of a pious,
innocent and tender mind.

Furnivall is (as one would expect) upon
Mrs Jameson's side. *He* reckons Isabella as
"the first of the three splendid women who
illumine the dark Third Period: she, glorious for her purity and righteousness, Cordelia for her truth and filial love, Volum-
nia for her devotion to honour and her love
of her native land. Perhaps we may add a
fourth, Portia, Brutus's wife, for nobleness
and wifely duty. But the highest of all is
Isabella." On the other hand Hazlitt is "not
greatly enamoured of Isabella's rigid chastity, though she could not have acted otherwise than she did. We do not feel the same
confidence in the virtue that is 'sublimely
good' at another's expense as if it had been
put to some less disinterested trial." And a
recent critic, Sir George Greenwood,
writes [2]:

Let Isabella be a paragon of virtue. Let her
chastity be as ice that no warmth of affection can
raise above the freezing-point, even though a dear

[2] In *The New World*, Nov. 1920.

brother's life may depend on it; let her be saint-
like, and virginal, and holy. But surely she might
reprove a wretched brother, lying in the valley of
the shadow of death, in restrained and measured
language, "more in sorrow than in anger," and
not with the abuse and vituperation of a terma-
gant!

We do not set ourselves up for umpires
in this dispute. Our point is that the dispute
itself—the mere fact that intelligent readers
can hold such opposite views of a character
which, on the face of it, should be simplicity
itself—is proof that the play misses clear-
ness in portraying its most important character.

And our own sense of the play has to
admit the perplexity of Isabella. It has an-
noyed us so that at one time we were almost
driven to examine her and Angelo as two
pendent portraits or studies in the ugliness
of Puritan hypocrisy. We grant, however,
that she is honestly conceived as a heroine;
and further, if the reader will, that hers (as
opposed to Cassandra's in the original) was
the righteous choice. Still, it has to be ad-
mitted that she is something rancid in her
chastity; and, on top of this, not by any
means such a saint as she looks. To put it
nakedly, she is all for saving her own soul,
and she saves it by turning, of a sudden,
into a bare procuress. It is, as we have said
in our General Introduction, the vindica-
tion of such a genius as Shakespeare's that
it carries on and sustains an equal though
different appeal to various succeeding ages.
But it must take the rough with the smooth
on its way. To Isabella the supposed Friar
(the disguised Duke) would be a holy man:
and we are all acquainted with the sort of
woman who will commit herself to any
deed without question, if it be suggested by
a priest. It remains a fact that on the supposed Friar's suggestion, and with no
qualm of conscience, but with careful contrivance, Isabella substitutes Mariana for
herself in Angelo's bed. Her panegyrists
may excuse it: they cannot overlook it: and
to us, in our day, it looks as if this virgin
"enskied and sainted" had saved herself by

a trick which denudes her own chastity of all but chastity's conventional (or conventual) religious trappings; that she is chaste, even fiercely chaste, for herself, without quite knowing what chastity means. We tell ourselves this; anon, as we read, we repent having said it; and, a page or so later, we say it again—or at least that "We do not love thee, Isabel. The reason why we cannot tell. . . ."

We put aside the question whether she was a better or a worse woman in refusing to sacrifice her chastity to save a very dear brother's life. On this point Sir George Greenwood makes confession:

For myself, I greatly prefer the character of Cassandra [the Cassandra of Whetstone's story], who was willing at the last to endure all the shame and misery in order to save the life of the brother whom she loved—even as Monna Vanna was willing to sacrifice herself in order to save the town and citizens of Pisa—to the rigid inflexible "virtue" of Shakespeare's Isabella! Such is my own opinion, let those condemn it who will.

We do not condemn it: yet we have no doubt that it lay within Shakespeare's power, at its best, to create an Isabella who should make the refusal and yet keep our sympathy along with our admiration. In the play, as we have it, he has not done this; and the trouble, to our thinking, lies *in his failure to make Isabella a consistent character.*

An exemplar of chastity should at all events be consistent—or at all events consistent in chastity, that most definite of virtues. But in fact one never knows where to take this paragon. She will plead Claudio's lapse as a venial sin: at the first suggestion of her own sinning it is "O, you beast!"—but by-and-by, to escape this, she is mating a pair without wedlock; while at the end we are left to suppose that for herself mating is mainly a question of marriage-lines; and that, for a Duke, she will throw her novitiate head-dress over the mill. She can be eloquent—so eloquent! She will plead to Angelo for clemency, for mercy, in

words that melt the heart: yet when it comes to her own turn to pity and forgive, she casts her own brother from her remorselessly, and never speaks to him again—no, not when he is returned to her from the tomb. Her gift of taciturnity would seem to be no less wayward, spasmodic, unaccountable, than her gift of golden speech. But this play, like some others of Shakespeare's, has mysterious silences. Claudio says nothing at all in the final ἀναγνώρισις which either dumbfounds him equally with his sister or leaves the pair equally and mutually cold.[3] He has spoken his last words in 4.2., not ignobly: Isabella ends on a string of palpable sophistry. When the Duke lordly announces his intent to make her his bride—

> Dear Isabel,
> I have a motion much imports your good,
> Whereto if you'll a willing ear incline . . .
> What's mine is yours, and what is yours is mine—

she is dumb again. The curtain falls, and there is an end.

In effect, Isabella disappoints. The stage has been carefully set for her. Brothel and prison contribute their darkness, all Vienna is taxed of its vice, to throw into higher relief this white apparition from the cloister, shining in purity, corsletted in virtue.[4] Yet in effect she disappoints: for in effect she writes no lesson on the dark walls, as they teach none to her soul. The true human interest slides away from her contention with Angelo to her contention with her wretched brother: and when that is over (and we have felt that, though her conduct may be exemplary, her behaviour has been too hard), she does little benefit to anybody.

[3] We must remind ourselves, however, that a drama does not depend on the spoken word alone. On the stage a gaze of incredulity, a sob, a speechless shelter in a brother's embrace might well be more effective than any speech. . . .

[4] The "value" of this setting is perhaps most appreciated when missed. We appeal for confirmation to anyone who has witnessed a performance of *Measure for Measure* with the Overdone business left out.

After 3.1., while by no means "static"—she is, if anything, too busy—she has missed her chance, and thenceforward performs no real good nor learns aught. The child Marina in *Pericles* passes through the brothel in Mitylene and passes out, triumphant, bequeathing some light of her purity to those that sit in darkness. It has been a trial of Una. But for our true release from the stews of Vienna and their foetid atmosphere we turn not to Isabella. We turn rather to Mariana's moated garden beyond the walls, "its dejected mistress, its long listless, discontented days, when we hear only the voice of a boy broken off suddenly in the midst of one of the loveliest songs of Shakespeare or of Shakespeare's school"—a garden upon the dusk of which Isabella glides with something more sinuous than the innocence of a dove. Mariana has little to say: but Mariana feels as Isabella does not; and with her we have at least the craving to be free of that Viennese world in which Isabella, with her Friar-Duke, is too fatally at home, and destined to be at home for all her vows. As the old rhyme has it:

Oh that I were where I would be!
Then should I be where I am not:
For where I am there I must be,
And where I would be I can not.

Is it extravagant to suppose that Shakespeare invented this remote and exquisite scene, with its sob of the lute, on realising that Isabella had failed, and was henceforth issueless, to deliver the spirit of his dream?

The Duke comports himself no less capriciously. He begins well, and in his exhortation to Claudio upon death he speaks most nobly. But he tails off into a stage-puppet and ends a wearisome man, talking rubbish. From the first no one quite knows why he has chosen to absent himself ostentatiously from Vienna and to come back pretending to be somebody else. His game puzzles Lucio only less completely than it puzzles us. The one thing certain about him, apart from the occasional nobility of his diction, is that, as guardian of the state and its laws, he shirks his proper responsibility and steals back *incognito* to play busy-body and spy on his deputy. This is Angelo's best excuse: that, for the play's purpose, his master knows either too much or too little of his antecedents. The amount of that knowledge, or of that suspicion, in one place contradicts the amount in another. We content ourselves here with one passage (3.1.159). The disguised Duke says to Claudio:

Son, I have overheard what hath passed between you and your sister. . . . Angelo had never the purpose to corrupt her; only he hath made an assay of her virtue, to practise his judgement with the disposition of natures. . . . She, having the truth of honour in her, hath made him that gracious denial which he is most glad to receive: I am confessor to Angelo, and I know this to be true.

Now this is a statement contrary to fact: but it is worse. It either betrays a priest's confessional secrecy or it is a flat falsehood. It is, for choice, a flat and unashamed falsehood—for how in a few hours could a sham priest have become Angelo's confessor? But whether a flat falsehood or a betrayal of holy confidence, it scarcely becomes the conscience of a Duke.

More and more, after the grand exhortation in 3.1., he seems to forget his own noble assurance in the opening scene:

Spirits are not finely touched
But to fine issues.

Yet we could forgive, while regretting, that his issues, and Isabella's, fail in fineness and end in staginess, if they were but pursued consistently with character. But they are not. They are pursued capriciously: and this, we suspect—albeit he did not go on to lay his instinct in account with reason—lurks beneath Hazlitt's complaint that "there may be said to be a general system of cross-purposes between the feelings of the different characters and the sympathy of the reader or the audience."

For, as Aristotle was at pains to point out long ago, above all things we require of a drama that its actions should follow one another in a sequence of necessity or probability, and that, to this end, *A* or *B* shall say or do, at any given moment, what he or she would naturally say or do. For the moment, by divination of genius, their author will make them say or do something which startles us: but the next instant we recognise it as right and natural and pay him our handsomest tribute, telling ourselves "Why, of course—but how did we miss to guess that *this* was coming—nay, bound to come?" Understanding—imaginative understanding—rules all drama, author conveying it to audience, from Oedipus' ἰὼ Κιθαιρών, τί μ' ἐδέχου; to Pompey Bum's "Truly, sir, I am a poor fellow that would live." Oedipus or Pompey, they must alike evoke the response in us, "There, but for the grace of God, go I."

M. C. Bradbrook

Authority, Truth, and Justice in *Measure for Measure*

Judge not, that ye be not judged.
For with what judgment ye judge, ye shall be judged: and with what measure ye mete it shall be measured to you again. (*Matthew*, VII. i–ii.)

THIS play is more theoretical than most of Shakespeare's writings, less easy, without his accustomed refusal to theorise or analyse. It differs from *Troilus and Cressida*, the problems of which are epistemological, and the method therefore impersonal but elaborate. In *Measure for Measure* the problems are ethical, and concern conduct rather than belief: the style is barer, sharper, and harder, the language simpler and plainer, and the characters allegorical rather than symbolical. The method, however, is akin to that of *Troilus and Cressida* in being largely based upon the debate: not the massed public debate, but the naked antagonism of conflict, as between Isabel and Angelo, Claudio and Isabel, and Claudio and the Duke.

In this play Shakespeare adopts a technique as analytic as that of Donne to something resembling the late medieval Morality.[1] It might be named The Contention between Justice and Mercy, or False Authority unmasked by Truth and Humility; Angelo stands for Authority and for Law, usurping the place of the Duke, who is not only the representative of Heavenly Justice but of Humility, whilst Isabel represents both Truth and Mercy.

The first necessity is to grasp the importance of the Duke. Historically he belongs to a familiar dramatic type; that of the om-

nipotent disguised character [2] who directs the intrigue, often hearing strange things of himself by the way—the type of Malevole, Vindice, the husband in *Eastward Ho!* and the father in *Englishmen for My Money*, a type to which the early Hamlet perhaps also belonged. Wilson Knight sees in him a Christlike figure come from a far country to save Vienna [3]: all powerful, all merciful, and perhaps in his marriage to Isabel only ratifying her position as the Bride of the Church. It is certain that the Duke is more than the average disguised puppet master of which Brainworm is the best known example: he is at least the representative of Heavenly Justice.

> I perceiue, your grace, like powre diuine
> Hath look'd vpon my passes.[4]

says Angelo. But as the play was written for performance at Court in 1604, it is possible that he also represents that pillar of justice, the British Solomon, James I, still in the first flush of popularity. Several compliments to his humility and dislike of crowds are palpably meant for the ear of James (I. i. 67–72; II. iv. 28–31).

No idea was more stressed by Elizabethan playwrights than that Justice lay in the hands of the magistrate,[5] as God's vice-

---

[1] Critics as different as Wilson Knight in *The Wheel of Fire* (1930) and R. W. Chambers in *Man's Unconquerable Mind* (1939) have treated *Measure for Measure* as primarily a study of ethics in terms of the Christian faith.

[2] See V. O. Freeburg, *Disguise Plots in Elizabethan Drama* (Columbia University Press, 1915); P. V. Kreider, "Mechanics of Disguise in Shakespeare's Plays," *Shakespeare Association Bulletin*, IX, 1934, 167–80; and *Comic Conventions in Chapman* (Michigan, 1935), Chapter III.

[3] III. ii. 235; v. i. 313–4.

[4] v. i. 370–1.

[5] See L. B. Campbell, "Theories of Revenge in Renaissance England" (*Modern Philology*, 1931) and F. T. Bowers, *Elizabethan Revenge Tragedy* (Milford, 1940).

Reprinted from the *Review of English Studies*, XVII (October 1941), 385–99, by permission of the Clarendon Press, Oxford.

gerent on earth. Hence Lord Chancellor Bacon deprecated Revenge, "a kind of wild justice," even in cases where the magistrate cannot or will not act.

As the Duke represents unerring Justice, and in his readiness to live as a poor Friar, helping his meanest and most criminal subjects, represents also Humility as it resides in true authority; so Isabel stands for unerring Truth, and Truth is always merciful.

> How would you be,
> If he which is the top of Iudgement should
> But iudge you, as you are?   (II. ii. 75–7)

she asks Angelo. The marriage of Truth and Justice resolves the frenzy of lies, prevarications, truths and half-truths which in the last scene records the hollowness of all external judgment, even as in *The Faerie Queene*, the marriage of Truth and Holiness, in the persons of Una and the Red Cross Knight, defeats the calumnious and evil forces represented by Duessa and Archimago.

Angelo stands for the letter of the Law, for a false Authority: he also stands for Seeming or False Semblant. At the very moment he is about to tempt Isabel he says:

> I (now the voyce of the recorded Law)
> Pronounce a sentence on your Brothers life.
>   (II. iv. 62–3)

But Authority is arbitrary (why pick out Claudio?), it apes a state unfit for humanity, encourages hidden vice in its own representative by endowing him with arbitrary power, and strives to overthrow truth and justice.[6]

Claudio and Juliet stand for human nature, original sin; Mariana for *eros* (as distinct from *agape*); Barnadine is contrasted with Claudio to show how much below panic-struck egoism is mere brute insensibility. Juliet, whom Claudio "wrong'd," is penitent from the first and therefore absolved by the Duke; nor apparently does she ever stand in peril of her life, and she is not given a judgment in the final scene as all the others are.[7] In the last scene measure for measure is meted out to all; not, perhaps, their measure according to earthly law—for Barnadine is pardoned—but the measure best devised to save their souls. The main purpose of the scene is to bring Angelo to repentance, and to achieve it against so strong a character terrific pressure has to be brought to bear. The Duke, who is as ruthlessly efficient in his means as he is benevolent in his ends, proceeds to apply the third degree with the skill of a Grand Inquisitor: and to this end he is ready to inflict any temporary suffering on Mariana and Isabel. Had they known his purpose they would have accepted the situation readily—Isabel from charity and Mariana from affection. Before the scene opens, Isabel complains that she must dissemble—"I would say the truth" (IV. vi. 2)—but the friar has told her it is "bitter to sweet end." The technique is only an advance upon the enacted lie of Mariana's visit, and that the Duke has justified beforehand: "Craft against vice I must applie" (III. ii. 299). He is naturally a merciful character; in theory he can condemn Barnadine, but when he actually sees the murderer, "A creature unpre-par'd, vnmeet for death," he realizes "To transport him in the minde he is, Were damnable" (IV. iii. 75–6). It is not Shakespeare's relenting before the miracle of his own creation, as the critics have sometimes stated, which reprieves Barnadine—in this play Shakespeare is hardly in a relenting mood—but the Duke's instinctive revolt from applying the penalties

---

[6] *Authority*: I. ii. 129; I. iv. 56; II. ii. 118, 134, 176; IV. ii. 114; IV. iv. 7, 27.

[7] Perhaps she is not really meant to appear. The stage directions are in very bad condition; and it seems likely that Juliet and Mariana might otherwise be doubled by the same boy, thus emphasizing their likeness as characters. They seem to have been in similar positions as regards their marriage contracts. See below. In the original story Juliet was required to wear "some disguised Apparel," i.e. a mark of infamy comparable to that worn by the heroine of Hawthorne's *Scarlet Letter*.

of the law without regard to their conse-
quences. He gives Barnadine to Friar Peter
to receive religious instruction, for he anticipates the maxim of Kant, and considers
every human being as an end and never as
a means, whether a means to the demonstration of the law or to other ends.

The debate between Justice and Mercy,
which is the main theme of the play—see
especially II. ii. and v. i.[8]—is conducted
mainly between Isabel and Angelo, for of
the Duke it might be said as it was of
archetype and ectype in *The Faerie Queene:*

> He merciful is, but Mercy's self is she.
> (cf. *F.Q.* II. ix. 43)

This debate can also be seen as a debate
between Law and Religion, of which Angelo and Isabel are by profession the rep-
resentatives. The Duke as secular head of
the state is bound to punish not only offences but the offenders: yet Christianity,
which he also professes, bids condemnation
of the sin, not the sinner. "Judge not that
ye be not judged. . . ." "Forgive us our
trespasses. . . ." "Unto seventy times sev-
en. . . ." The two sides of his dilemma
are stated by Isabel and Angelo:

> I haue a brother is condemn'd to die,
> I doe beseech you let it be his fault,
> And not my brother. . . .
> Condemne the fault, and not the actor of it,
> Why, euery fault's condemnd ere it be done:
> Mine were the verie Cipher of a Function. . . .
> (II. ii 34–9)

On the other hand, Angelo's "devilish mercy" is, as the Duke sees, the very converse
of true forgiveness:

> When Vice makes Mercie; Mercie's so extended,
> That for the faults loue, is th' offender friended.
> (IV. ii. 115–6)

Yet Isabel pardons Angelo when he is for-
feit to the law, and asks the Duke to pardon

[8] *Justice:* I. i. 11; I. ii. 132; I. iii. 29, 32; II. i.
21–30; II. ii. 41, 76, 100, 177; II. iv. 53; III. ii.
263–4, 275; IV. i. 75; IV. ii. 83, 89, 101, 199; v. i.
6, 20, 25, 27, 54, 159, 166, 288, 297, 308, 310, 444,
473. *Mercy:* II. i. 306; II. ii 50, 60–3, 78; III. i. 63,
148; IV. ii. 115; v. i. 408, 435, 477, 485.

him also. The Duke deliberately reminds
her of the *lex talionis*, as well as appealing
to all her feelings of rage and resentment:
"He dies for *Claudio's* death" (v. i. 444).
Yet although Isabel's first and natural impulse on hearing of her brother's execution
had been "Oh, I wil to him, and plucke out
his eies!" she kneels "in mercy of this
fact," and perhaps it is this, rather than
any of the Duke's ingenious tortures,
which finally breaks the spirit of Angelo,
though—an exquisite touch—only to the
applying of his own legal standard to himself.

> And so deepe . . . sticks it in my penitent
> heart,
> That I craue death more willingly then mercy,
> 'Tis my deseruing, and I doe entreat it.
> (v. i. 476–8)

The retributive aspect of criminal law
seems always to have distressed Shakespeare. The cry of the tragedies is "None
does offend, I say: none," and in the final
plays the penalties of the law are waived
for the most flagrant evil-doers—Iachimo,
Alonzo, Sebastian. The problem that a
law to be just in general, must always be
only an approximation to justice in particular cases, is stressed both by Claudio
who suffers under it and the Duke who ad-
ministers it.

> On whom it will, it will,
> On whom it will not (soe) yet still tis iust.
> (I. ii. 131–2)

> Lawes, for all faults,
> But faults so countenanc'd, that the strong Stat-
> utes
> Stand like the forfeites in a Barbers shop,
> As much in mocke, as marke. (v. i. 317–20)

Yet here as in other plays Law in the
sense of civil law is a constant subject of
praise. Ulysses' speech in defence of order
and degree (*Troilus and Cressida* I. iii) is
the most comprehensive eulogy, with its
assimilation of human institutions, contracts and laws to the universal order of
times and seasons. In *Henry IV, Part II*,
the Lord Chief Justice stands as the em-

bodiment of everything that's excellent, and clearly represents civil law. He is the real antagonist of Falstaff, and it is he whom King Henry V admits as "a father to my youth" (v. ii. 118) after the judge has made his noble defence of his own act in committing to prison "the immediate heir of England."

> I then did vse the Person of your Father . . .
> Your Highnesse pleased to forget my place,
> The Maiesty, and power of Law, and Iustice,
> The Image of the King, whom I presented,
> And strooke me in my very Seate of Iudge-
> ment. . . .   (v. ii. 73 ff.)

This adoption seals the doom of Falstaff, the grey-haired iniquity who was even then saying, "The Lawes of England are at my command'ment. Happie are they, which haue been my Friendes: and woe vnto my Lord Chief Iustice!" (v. iii. 140-3).

No doubt for the purposes of the stage the Lord Chief Justice walked around in Eastcheap in full robes of office, and he is in a sense the pivot of the play, Henry IV being shown as a weak and dying man, a father rather than a king.

In *Measure for Measure* civil law enters the story chiefly through the marriage contracts. Juliet and Mariana are both contracted: Claudio says,

> Vpon a true contract
> I got possession of *Iulietas* bed,
> You know the Lady, she is fast my wife,
> Saue that we doe the denunciation lacke
> Of outward Order. . . .   (I. ii. 155-9)

which was deferred for financial reasons. It is not clear whether this was a marriage "per verba de praesenti," as was the Duchess of Malfi's; if so, the child would be legitimate, as the union was customary, and neither party could have married elsewhere according to the English law and habit.[9]

[9] See C. L. Powell, *English Domestic Relations*, 1487-1653 (Columbia U.P., 1917), ch. I. "Spousals *de praesenti* were . . . vows made similarly to the *de futuro* but in the present tense, and were in effect, though not in name, absolute marriage. They could be broken only by death or by entrance into holy orders. In case of cohabitation

Nevertheless the marriage was not regular, and in Chapman's continuation of *Hero and Leander* it may be seen what immense stress was laid on the public nature of the marriage contract, both in the vision of the goddess Ceremony, who descends to rebuke Hero, and in the Tale of Teras, which is a glorification of the social aspect of marriage.

Mariana was publicly affianced "as strongly as words could make up vows" (v. i. 220-1), and the marriage settlements had been actually drawn up. Angelo is therefore her "combynate husband," and the Duke envisages that the result of their union may be a child whose existence will "compell him to her recompense" (III. i. 263-4). The fact that the contract had been public and approved by the lady's friends would weigh very strongly with the Elizabethans, for to steal a marriage was almost a misdemeanour, as the case of the Duchess of Malfi demonstrated.

Isabella is the Bride of the Church, and to the horror of proposed violation Angelo adds a direct crime against religion. As a novice she is as it were betrothed, and apparently on the eve of her "approbation." If she were a novice she would be subject to the authority of the Mother, would wear the novice's dress, and obey the Rule, which was that of the Poor Clares, an order of great poverty, seclusion, and austerity, re-

after either form of spousals, without any marriage ceremony, the offenders laid themselves open to punishment by the Church, but their union was recognised as a valid marriage by both church and state. It was thus possible to contract an irregular but perfectly legal marriage without the sanction or the intervention of either civil or ecclesiastical authority" (pp. 3-4). For a briefer account see A. Underhill, art. "Law" in *Shakespeare's England*, i, pp. 407-8.

In *The Miseries of Inforct Marriage*, Clare regards her spousals to Scarborow as a binding union and her subsequent marriage as adulterous. In Ford's *Broken Heart*, Penthea thinks that "her name is strumpeted" because while betrothed to Orgilus, her brother has forced her to marry Bassanes.

formed into still further strictness by the work of St. Colette (*c.* 1400) and the Capuchines (*c.* 1540). Isabel's vows should have been taken between her first and second interview with Angelo; in the second, she is introduced as "One *Isabell, a Sister,*" and the friar addresses her as "sister," in iii. I, a term he would not use to a novice; but if in the interval she had been given the first veil—it is scarcely likely that she was at a more advanced stage—she would hardly accuse herself publicly of incontinence, considering the disgrace to her order. It seems more reasonable that she should defer her vows, and that in the last scene she should appear in secular clothes, perhaps in mourning for Claudio. The Duke also appears again in secular habit, and changes of clothes had a strong effect upon the Elizabethan stage. An Isabel in a secular habit could be arrested with more propriety than an Isabel in a veil; and the final tableau also would look less unnatural.

Some indication of the Elizabethan view of marriage as a public contract rather than a private relationship may be gained, as has been said, from Chapman; though English youth was more free than that of most countries, the rule was still that marriage should be determined by social equality, family duty, and public advantage rather than by personal inclination. Juliet and Mariana are parallel in misfortune: in the view of the friar Juliet is more guilty than Claudio, but in the view of Isabel the sin is Claudio's:

Women? Helpe heauen: men their creation marre
In profiting by them: Nay, call us ten times fraile,
For we are soft, as our complexions are,
And credulous to false prints. (II. iv. 128–31)

It is the old story, "Men have marble, women waxen minds," and their fatal vulnerability lies in their sympathetic natures: they lack judgment and intellectual detachment. Hence even the Duke adjures

Claudio to marry her he has "wrong'd," and he insists on a full marriage ceremony for Mariana to "safe-guard" her "honor" against "Imputation" (v. i. 420–3). Even Lucio, though forgiven for his other forfeits, is obliged to make an honest woman of Mistress Kate Keepdown. The four marriages represent, in descending order of dignity, variations upon this basic social contract. In *The Merchant of Venice*, a forerunner of this play in so many ways, the marriage contract is symbolized in the story of the rings, and contrasted with Shylock's purely legal bond. Marriage is the highest form of contract, in that it contains subtler possibilities for good, for evil, for variety than other types of contract: it not only imposes a legal obligation, but contains a promise of personal and general prosperity of the highest kind.

The basis of Justice and of Law is the establishment of truth. Perfect truth resides only in God: the devil is the father of lies, and in the current morality representations of him, his power of disguise, particularly of disguising himself as a virtue, was his subtlest weapon for the destruction of man.[10] Hence the question of Truth apparent and real, of Falsehood conscious and unconscious is crucial to the plot. Shakespeare had before him the great visionary panorama of the first book of *The Faerie Queene*. This problem he had himself approached in *King Henry IV, Part II*, where the Prologue is spoken by Rumour "painted full of tongues." Rumour sets the tone for the play by appearing in this fashion: her nearest modern equivalent would be the Fairy Wish-Fulfilment. But the question of

[10] Moralities persisted into the seventeenth century: e.g. *The Contention of Liberality and Prodigality* was acted before the Queen in 1602 (see Hazlitt's Dodsley, *A Collection of Old English Plays*, vol. viii). For an account of the later Tudor Moralities, see Louis B. Wright in *Anglia*, vol. LIV; and for the disguising of evil characters see W. R. Mackenzie, *The English Morality Play from the Point of View of Allegory* (Boston, 1914), p. 9. See also E. S. N. Thompson, *The English Moral Play* (Connecticut Academy of Arts and Sciences, vol. 14, 1910).

"Where lies Truth?" is not overtly debated. The contrast between True and False Seeming is stronger and more painful in *Troilus and Cressida*, where the whole tragedy of "True Troilus" turns on the gap between fact and imagination, Diomede's Cressida and his own: "If there be rule in unitie itselfe, This is not she." In *Measure for Measure*, the issue is prominent, but it is not a subject for debate or doubt. The main contrast between seeming and reality lies of course in "the prenzie Angelo," "the well-seeming Angelo," "this outward-sainted deputy." The Duke's first speech is an ironic comment on this:

> There is a kinde of Character in thy life
> That to th' obsseruer, doth thy history
> Fully vnfold.   (I. i. 27–8)

But it is made plain in the next scene but one that the Duke is by no means reading Angelo's life in the accepted version.[11]

The "seeming" of the deputy is echoed so often and so bitterly that to dwell on it would be tedious.[12] Angelo has in him something of the dissembling power of Claudius King of Denmark, and also of his gnawing conscience; he is "At warre, twixt will and will not."[13] Isabel, who, like Hamlet, "knows not 'seems'" but is forced to learn it, maintains the truth although Angelo's false outweighs her true: "Truth is truth To th' end of reckning" (v. i. 44–5). After describing Angelo's "seeming," she concludes to the Duke:

[11] I. iii. 50–54. Cf. the words of Duncan, "There's no Art, To finde the Mindes construction in the Face" (*Macbeth*, I. iv. 11–12), and of Malcolm, "Angels are bright still, though the brightest fell. Though all things foule, would wear the brows of grace Yet Grace must still looke so" (IV. iii. 22–24).

[12] Angelo's *Seeming*: I. i. 66; I. iii. 54; II. iv. 15, 147, 151; III. i. 231; III. ii. 40–1; v. i. 52–7. The mood is that of Sonnet xciv: "They that have power to hurt and will do none," with its terrible last line, "Lilies that fester smell far worse than weedes."

[13] II. ii. 33. Cf. II. iv. 1–17, and *Hamlet*, III. iii. 36–66.

> Let your reason serue
> To make the truth appeare, where it seemes hid,
> And hide the false seemes true.   (v. i. 65–7)

She is traduced as sorely as the Duke had been traduced by Lucio: yet she remains steadfast, more steadfast than the Duke would have been, for to him, as to Prospero, life itself is a dream and all its events but "seeming."[14]

> Thou hast nor youth, nor age
> But as it were an after-dinners sleepe
> Dreaming on both.   (III. i. 32–4)

Yet the Duke is capable of turning every occasion to his own purpose, as in his ironic speech to Angelo on his return, which is designed to give a smart lash to the conscience of the deputy, and to express his own scepticism on "the vanity of wretched fooles."

> Giue me your hand,
> And let the Subiect see, to make them know
> That outward curtesies would faine proclaime
> Fauours that keepe within.   (v. i. 13–16)

On two occasions the Duke is surprised: he did not expect that Angelo would have Claudio executed, and he did not expect Isabel, to whom he had promised "revenges to your heart" (IV. iii. 144), to forgive Angelo, though with his usual keenness he immediately seizes the opportunity to test the depth of her impulse.

Angelo himself upheld the doctrine of seeming. He admits to Escalus that a jury may contain worse criminals than the prisoner it condemns, yet the known crime must be punished.

> What knowes the Lawes
> That theeues do passe on theeues?
>   (II. i. 22–3)

But, he continues,

> When I, that censure him, do so offend,
> Let mine owne Iudgement patterne out my
>   death.   (II. i. 29–30)

[14] The comparison between Claudio on death, and Hamlet, "To be or not to be," has often been noticed.

In this alone Angelo is not a seemer; he has the consistency to sentence himself.

> Immediate sentence then, and sequent death,
> Is all the grace I beg.   (v. i. 374-5)

In his fate, the Elizabethans would recognize the best and indeed the only true justice, that which is invoked by the title: Heaven's justice or Providence. They believed that justice could be left to the magistrate because if he were unable or unwilling to execute it, Heaven would deal justice to the evil-doer. Whoever else forgot his contract God would not, and "Vengeance is mine, I will repay, saith the Lord." [15]

The Duke, in his own way, is as great a seemer as Angelo. In his role as a poor Friar he is continually placed in ironic situations, his real and his seeming character being perpetually brought into conflict by unconscious words of Isabella, Escalus, the Provost and Lucio—such phrases as "But (oh) how much is the good Duke deceiu'd in *Angelo:* if euer he returne, and I can speake to him, I will open my lips in vaine, or discouer his gouernment" (III. i. 195-8). Some of the situations the Duke enjoys [16] and more he turns to good account, but on one occasion he is rudely disillusioned. He had at least believed that the people loved him, and had retired only to preserve his reputation with them; yet he learns with cruel elaboration from Lucio how little a public man can claim immunity from slander. He is almost driven, in forgetfulness of his habit and his office alike, to challenge Lucio:

[15] This fact is a central theme in Revenge Tragedy and examples may be found in L. B. Campbell, and F. T. Bowers, *op. cit.* In particular, Tourneur's *Revenger's Tragedy* shows the corruption of earthly justice and the inevitability of heaven's redress. Cf. *Hamlet:* "I am justly killed with mine owne Treacherie" (v. ii. 321); *King Lear:* "The Wheele is come full circle; I am heere" (v. iii. 176); *Macbeth:* "This euen-handed Iustice Commends th' Ingredience of our poyson'd Challice To our owne lips" (I. vii. 10-12).
[16] There are at least three stories as to why the friar is absent in v. i—he is sick, constrained by a vow, gone away.

> *Duke.* . . . I am bound to call vppon you, and
> I pray you your name?
> *Lucio.* Sir my name is *Lucio,* wel known to the
> Duke.   (III. ii. 171-3)

In the last scene he suffers defamation from the same quarter in his person as a friar, when Lucio coolly puts into his own mouth all the slanders which he had been obliged to listen to. The Duke is wounded in his one vulnerable point, the dignity of his office, and it requires a second thought before he can pardon Lucio.

The difference between the Duke's seeming and that of Angelo is of course that the Duke's is purely an external change. In one sense he is a benevolent Haroun-al-Raschid; but his purposes are better than mere curiosity, and he is not defaming the cloak of religion.

> Come hither *Isabell.*
> Your *Frier* is now your Prince: As I was then,
> Aduertysing, and holy to your businesse,
> (Not changing heart with habit) I am still,
> Atturnied at your seruice.   (v. i. 382-6)

He who was greatest has been as a servant amongst them.

In the actions of Angelo, Isabel, and the Duke, the question of Truth and Seeming is stated, and they have thus a double burden of symbolism to carry. Nevertheless, the allegorical nature of *Measure for Measure* does not preclude a human interest in the characters. Though based perhaps on the Moralities, it is not a Morality. Angelo has always been recognized as a superb character study; Isabel and the Duke, though less impressive, are subtly presented. She is possibly the most intelligent of all Shakespeare's women; even poor Claudio recognizes her power in "reason and discourse" (I. ii. 196); yet she is young, and pitifully inexperienced. Outraged by Angelo's proposal, she turns to Claudio, the only man to whom she can turn—to ask for comfort as much as to give it:

> Ile to my brother,
> Though he hath falne by prompture of the
> blood,
> Yet hath he in him such a minde of Honor. . . .
>   (II. iv. 178-80)

But Claudio gives her an even crueller shock than Angelo had done, though to the eye of the spectator he is not without a case. He had had to listen to poor Isabel's bungled attempts at religious consolation. "Dar'st thou die? . . ." she says, galling the sorest point with intolerable accuracy; and whereas the friar had persuaded Claudio to at least temporary resignation, Isabella's efforts to "fit his mind to death" make him snarl very excusably:

> Why giue you me this shame?
> Think you I can a resolution fetch
> From flowrie tendernesse?   (III. i. 79–81)[17]

Yet it is the same girl who cries to Claudio, "Die, perish!" and who cries, when he is in all appearance dead, for revenge on Angelo: "Oh, I wil to him, and plucke out his eics!" It is the same girl to whom Mariana appeals for help—

> They say best men are moulded out of faults—

and at that word Isabel, who not five minutes before had called Angelo a devil, recalls Claudio, recalls her own position as a suppliant for a dear but guilty life, and astounds even that skilled psychologist the Duke. Impulsively she kneels: intelligently she at once proceeds to justify the action.[18] The garden house affair was after all an attempt to bribe Angelo, and he did not break the law in disregarding that illegal contract: "My Brother had but Iustice, In that he did the thing for which he dide." Whilst to the Duke, who had himself prevented Angelo's worst crime, she points out that Angelo is innocent before the law with respect to herself. It is a legal quibble

worthy of Portia, and devised with the same speed as the sudden attempt to turn Angelo's attack upon herself to advantage:

> Signe me a present pardon for my brother,
> Or with an out-stretcht throate Ile tell the world aloud
> What man thou art.   (II. iv. 153–5)

But while there the answer had been "Who will beleeue thee *Isabell*" (II. iv. 155), here justice recognizes, as Isabel points it out, the one grain of good in Angelo:[19] "A due sinceritie governed his deedes, Till he did looke on me" (v. i. 447–8). Having been overruled with regard to Angelo, the Duke proceeds to pardon Barnadine, Claudio, Lucio—though somewhat more reluctantly—and everybody else.

The Duke himself is a type of character whom Shakespeare did not often depict. His relations with his people are comparable with those of Henry V with Bates and Williams—Williams in particular is left rather in the position of Lucio; and, like Henry V, he can be extremely peremptory, is a born administrator, and enjoys probing and investigating into the lives of the common people—he would have appreciated Prince Hal's conversation with the drawer. On the other hand he more resembles Prospero in that all his actions are controlled by one purpose, in that complete self-confidence justifies his seeming cruelties (compare Prospero to Ferdinand), and in his almost unerring moral insight—being only twice deceived or surprised by other people's reactions. He resembles Prospero also in the absolute power which he maintains over the lives of the rest of the characters, except indeed the minor comic characters. These, the human sediment of Vienna, are not capable of being systematized: they exist independently of the moral framework and help further to give the

---

[17] The Duke restores Claudio's resolution by the cool falsehood that Angelo is only testing Isabel's virtue. Many critics have rebuked him for this unducal behaviour. But the aim is to prepare Claudio for a Christian death: the Duke lies promptly *for this end*.

[18] The antithesis of Angelo's appalling deliberation in taking the curb off his impulses: "Now I giue my sensuall race the reine" (II. iv. 161).

[19] "Loue talks with better knowledge, and knowledge with dearer loue" (III. ii. 163–4), as the Duke says. Truth alone can be truly charitable and charity alone can discern truth completely.

play its naturalism and solidity. The difference between Pompey and Barnadine is the
difference between a character and a por-
tent—between the Artful Dodger and Bill
Sikes.

In respect of the style, as of the plot, the
structural pattern of main themes does not
inhibit local energy, especially in the first
part of the play. There are several images
that run through the play, e.g. the "hidden
ulcer"—the dominant image of *Hamlet:*
this is as it were the physical equivalent of
the False Semblant, which skins and films
the ulcerous places. There are also the images of great heat and cold: Angelo's blood
is "Snow-broth"; Claudio fears the intense
cold, the "thrilling Region of thicke-
ribbed Ice" which may receive his soul
after death; but on the whole there is comparatively little imagery after the third act.
The acting possibilities of the latter half of
the play are great; but it depends upon
repetition and cross references. The nature
of the writing here is fairly represented by
Isabel's plea to the Duke. Angelo, accusing
her of madness, says "she will speake most
bitterly, and strange":

> *Isabel.* Most strange: but yet most truely wil
>   I speake,
> That *Angelo's* forsworne, is it not strange?
> That *Angelo's* a murtherer, is't not strange?
> That *Angelo* is an adulterous thiefe,
> An hypocrite, a virgin violator,
> Is it not strange? and strange?
>   *Duke.*   Nay it is ten times strange?
> *Isabel.* It is not truer he is *Angelo,*
> Then this is all as true, as it is strange;
> Nay, it is ten times true, for truth is truth
> To th' end of reckning.   (v. i. 37–46)

As conventional rhetoric depending on ana-
phora and epiphora, this is reminiscent of
Constance or the Lady Anne rather than of
the language of Shakespeare's maturity.
However, it fits the dramatic situation—Isabel is almost in the position of a prosecut-
ing counsel—and her own natural anger—
she plays with the Duke's phrase as bitterly
as she does with Angelo's. Beyond this, the
full values of "true" and "strange," as they

chime through the speech like the rhymes
of a canzone, depend upon this being the
finale of a great movement; the phrases
take their value from their previous use,
and the broad treatment here given to them
is only possible because their full implications have been already worked out. This
is more definitely illustrated in the Duke's
consolation to Isabel for Claudio's supposed death.

> That life is better life past fearing death,
> Then that which liues to feare: make it your
>   comfort,
> So happy is your Brother   (v. i. 398–400)

he says, condensing his great speech in
III. i. to an epigram.

The flattening out of the language in the
latter half of this play is similar to the
flattening out in *The Jew of Malta*, where
Marlowe also began in a style rich and flex-
uous with imagery, and ended with a bare,
"figurative," and comparatively prosaic
speech. *Measure for Measure* remains a
problem play, not because it is shallower,
more unfinished or more incoherent than
Shakespeare's other plays, but because it
is stiffened by its doctrinaire and impersonal consideration of ethical values. The
dryness, the pain behind the play, seem to
depict a world in which external personal
relationships are so hopelessly false and un-
reliable that it is necessary to cut below
them to the moral substratum.[20] To look for
happiness is childish: what should be
looked for is the good, proper, socially fitting relation; the basis is impersonal morality.

The relationships between justice and
mercy, contract and fulfilment, appearance
and reality are summed up in the relationship between earthly and heavenly justice;
between the Duke in his secular and religious roles; between Isabel as a sister to
her "vnhappie brother *Claudio,*" and the
bosom friend of Julietta, and Isabel as the

[20] This is the mood of Sonnets xciii, xciv, xcvi,
cxx, cxxi, cxlvii.

sister of St. Clare among the "fasting Maides, whose mindes are dedicate to nothing temporall." When the Duke asks her hand he invokes her human sisterhood:

> Giue me your hand, and say you will be mine,
> He is my brother too.   (v. i. 493-4)

It was a large charity in the Duke to accept Claudio, who is not exactly an eligible relative for the head of the state, and with whose failings he is particularly well acquainted. If this conclusion seem a trifle laboured in the working out, the play perhaps justifies it as the representation of a bitterness which could as yet find but little heart to conceive that triumph of the good which is most firmly asserted, and believed, but which was not to be fully embodied till eight years later in *The Tempest*. As a final check upon Shakespeare's intentions, it is of interest to see how he modified his source, Whetstone's *Promos and Cassandra* (1578).[21] He invented almost the entire role of the Duke—it is for this reason that the understanding of the Duke's character becomes especially necessary—for in Whetstone's play the King appears only in the final scene to deliver judgement. He split the heroine Cassandra into two characters, Isabel and Mariana; for in the original

Cassandra yields, comes to love Promos, in spite of his having seemingly presented her with the bleeding head of her brother, and finally pleads for his life because she loves him, and he is her husband. Shakespeare has made Isabel a nun, which adds a completely different complexion to Angelo's temptation: in Whetstone there are not only no religious characters, there is no invoking of any religious standards. Shakespeare has changed the story of Claudio, who as Andrugio was allowed to escape by the Provost, the Provost being alone responsible for the substituted head; in the final scene Andrugio delivers himself up to save Promos, in pity for his sister's misery. Finally, Shakespeare has added all the minor comic characters, and moralized the main story: adding, that is to say, the whole structure of themes. A careful comparison of Shakespeare's and Whetstone's plays is not required. Whetstone's is wretched drivel; but the baldest summary records how completely Shakespeare transformed a shallow and barbarous story. The purposive nature of these changes makes it seem very unlikely that *Measure for Measure* contains many accidental, idle or automatic incidents. If it is strange, it is because Shakespeare conceived it in that way. It is deliberately, if not dogmatically, set down. Perhaps its best commentator would have been Ben Jonson: it is one of the few of Shakespeare's writings of which he might wholeheartedly have approved.

[21] Editions by W. C. Hazlitt, *Shakespeare's Library*, vi. 201 (1875) and J. S. Farmer, *Tudor Facsimile Texts* (1910). The play is in two parts. The story comes from Giraldo Cinthio's *Hecatommithi* (also the source of *Othello*).

W. M. T. Dodds

The Character of Angelo in *Measure for Measure*

SIR ARTHUR QUILLER-COUCH has remarked [1] that in the treatment of Angelo Shakespeare "has indicated . . . a true soul's tragedy," but unfortunately this view is by no means universally accepted. The soul's tragedy in Angelo has been much neglected; Angelo is not commonly included in the gallery of great Shakespearean portraits. It seems that in literature as in life it is impossible fully to recover a reputation once lost:

> Stay (quoth Reputation)
> Doe not forsake me: for it is my nature
> If once I part from any man I meete,
> I am never found again: And so, for you:
> You have shooke hands with Reputation,
> And made him invisible: So fare you well.

The recoilings of nineteenth-century criticism have left their mark and accordingly in the twentieth century Angelo is suspect still. W. W. Lawrence writes, in his *Problem Comedies:*

> Did Shakespeare mean Angelo to be regarded as a good, though narrow, man, suddenly gone wrong through an overmastering sexual temptation? . . . Or was Angelo a villain from the start, who deceived the Duke as to his real character? I do not imagine there is any way of settling this point. [2]

Even where Angelo's probity before his fall is not questioned, the critic may remain openly hostile and speak, for example, of Angelo's

. . . self-righteous, humorless, pseudo-judicial stiffness. . . . It is a type of character frequently advanced to executive positions, where it enjoys

[1] In his Introduction to the New Cambridge Shakespeare edition of *Measure for Measure*, p. xlii.
[2] P. 113.

tyrannizing over less successful, more decent men. [3]

Either attitude is fatal to the true interpretation of Angelo's character. If he is seen either as dissembler or as prig, he cannot at the same time be seen as a man whose soul is large and fine enough to experience tragic intensity of suffering. It is the purpose of this study to aver that Angelo's spirit is indeed, as the Duke remarks, "finely touched," and to attend, in a detailed analysis, to the care and passion which Shakespeare lavished on this character—a care and passion not less than that given to a Macbeth or an Othello, but different in its manifestations.

More is at stake than merely the interpretation of one character. Angelo's part in the dramatic economy of *Measure for Measure* is an important one: he typifies strict justice. The contention between Angelo and Isabella is, as well as the personal issue, the greater issue of Justice and Mercy; it is therefore of crucial importance that the justice should be as genuine as the mercy. It is of course part of the argument of the play that the ministers of justice in this mortal life are fallible, but this does not (as Angelo explains to Escalus) reflect upon the quality of abstract Justice itself, and Shakespeare has taken great care to show Angelo as a man whose ideals of abstract Justice are clear, and to be revered, whatever his own practice as a "justicer" may be. To dismiss these ideals as narrow, priggish, pharisaical, is to destroy the dramatic antithesis upon which the argument turns. It is therefore vital to the understanding of

[3] Hazelton Spencer, *The Art and Life of William Shakespeare*, p. 302.

Reprinted from *Modern Language Review*, XLI (July 1946), 246–55, by permission of the Modern Humanities Research Association and the author, Mrs. W. M. T. Nowottny.

the play as a whole to put from oneself all hostility to the idea of Justice as typified by Angelo before his fall. It is a Christian commonplace to think of justice giving place to mercy, but it is unchristian to decry justice itself.

And indeed there is, at the root of erroneous interpretations of Shakespeare's conception of Angelo, a neglect of Christian thinking on the matter of sin. Christian experience has been that goodness carries no exemption, in this life, from the fury of the Tempter; no man is guaranteed against a sudden fall from grace. It is this truth which is neglected when we argue that Angelo tempting Isabel is Angelo revealing his true nature and that, therefore, the golden opinions he had won from the Duke were always unmerited. The case for branding Angelo dissembler rests on the supposition that nothing but a long course of covert sinning could have fitted him to make his bed in hell with such rapidity. Against that supposition stands the evidence of the play itself and in particular the evidence of the very scene in which Angelo tempts Isabel with the offer of her brother's life in return for the enjoyment of her person.

His own words to Isabel when the offer has been made:

> I have begun;
> And now I give my sensual race the rein:

are clearly the words of a man who knows himself to be embarking on a course he has so far eschewed, and Angelo is here speaking more to himself—passing a verdict on the morality of his own decisions, as was his custom—than to Isabel. But even if these words be discounted, as no more than the automatic excuses of a hypocrisy so finished as to plead first offence in the very moment of crime, there yet remains as evidence the whole tenour of Angelo's attempt to seduce.

The attempt is made by argument, and theological argument at that. A moment's reflection on a parallel scene by Ben Jonson (Volpone's temptation of Celia) will underline the importance of Shakespeare's treatment here. Volpone tempts Celia (whose answers indicate a piety no less entrenched than Isabel's) with visions of wealth and outspoken invitations to pleasures both lusty and recondite. Angelo reasons with Isabel's conscience, and it is a fair inference that his estimate of her nature is based on his knowledge of his own; he reasons with her because he cannot imagine that she will be brought to commit any action which her conscience does not first approve, any more than he would himself were it not that passion is now "dispossessing all [his] other parts of necessary fitness." If it be argued that this proceeds, not from the habits of a lifetime of deliberation on right conduct, but from a crafty assessment of his adversary's strength, one passage refutes the allegation. Angelo begins to argue that sins committed under compulsion have no gravamen:

> Our compelled sins
> Stand more for number than accompt

but immediately takes back the words, saying,

> Nay, I'll not warrant that; for I can speak
> Against the thing I say

Here, plainly, we have a man who cannot, even to compass his own ends, even while knowing himself to be on the way to mortal sin, bring himself to employ an argument which he himself knows to be false. For "hypocrisy" and "narrowness" of this calibre all scholars may well pray.

The truth is, of course, that Angelo is exactly as the Duke describes him: a man whose whole way of life bears on it the mark that enables an observer of men to reconstruct the secret history of self-discipline that has gone to its making.

> Angelo,
> There is a kind of character in thy life
> That to the observer doth thy history
> Fully unfold.

To aver that the Duke too was deceived by "seeming, seeming," and speaks with no authority, is to ignore the care that Shakespeare took in giving the Duke the vocabulary and style of a thinker and also Shakespeare's care in adding weight to the choice of Angelo for the supreme position, by making the Duke first commend and commission Escalus and then top commendation by preferring Angelo to the higher office. It is, also, to ignore Shakespeare's revelation of Angelo in his style of utterance.

There are two striking characteristics of Angelo's speech: one is the absence of that welling imagery associated, in Shakespeare's practice, with the presence of strong passions; the other is the frequency and nicety of the ethical distinctions Angelo makes.

Angelo thinks with concepts, not with impassioned images. The rare images he does use are deliberate illustrations of his thought and these are elaborated without change of metaphor, as in the lines

> We must not make a scarecrow of the law,
> Setting it up to fear the birds of prey,
> And let it keep one shape, till custom make it
> Their perch and not their terror.

This intellectual deployment of analogy, radically different from the maelstrom of imagery characteristic of a Macbeth, is no accident, for when Angelo is in the grip of his passion for Isabel the character of his speech changes, and the images which are no more than exempla give place to images jetted out by the spring of emotions within. A similar alternation can be studied in *The Winter's Tale:* when Hermione addresses Polixenes, the imagery is languid, is trotted out, and it is apparent there is none of the secret stress that Leontes later suspects, but when she addresses Leontes, her deep feeling for him suffuses her speech with metaphors melting the one into the other. Evidently, Shakespeare has taken care to give Angelo the imagery of a man in whom passion is not yet awake.

The frequency of ethical distinction in Angelo's speech needs only mention in order to be recognized. For example:

> Condemn the fault, and not the actor of it?
> Why, every fault's condemned, ere it be done.

> It is the law, not I, condemn your brother.

> The law hath not been dead, though it hath slept.

> [—*Isab*. Yet show some pity—]
> —I show it most of all, when I show justice,
> For then I pity those I do not know
> Which a dismissed offence would after gall.

The two things, the character of the imagery and the nicety of distinction, are unmistakeable in the argument with Escalus about the sentence on Claudio. Escalus has urged mercy on the grounds that Claudio succumbed to a universal temptation and that Angelo must have felt in himself the stirrings of the same vice. Angelo replies, with strict logic:

> 'Tis one thing to be tempted, Escalus,
> Another thing to fall,

and then demolishes the case that Escalus has put. Granted, the jury may contain some few who are guiltier than the prisoner they condemn, but the consideration is irrelevant, for two reasons: first, justice is concerned only with known facts ("what's open made to justice, that justice seizes"), secondly, justice is an impersonal autonomy which takes no cognizance of the human instruments who are its executors ("what know the laws that thieves do pass on thieves?"); both these points may easily be illustrated, the first by the analogy of the jewel lying on the ground—if seen, it is taken up, if not seen it is trodden on, though it remains in all cases a jewel; the second by taking the extreme case of partiality, that of a man for himself, and reflecting that even in that case justice is, ideally, so independent of its ministers that Angelo condemning Angelo would be logical, whereas Angelo pardoning Claudio because Angelo is guilty, would be absurd.

And it is typical of Angelo's mental habits that having stated a formed decision, he immediately sees it in terms of its issue in action: "Sir, he must die." This is the mark of effective thinking: the intention of achieving decision and promptly converting decision into fact. It is so in his treatment of Isabel. He attempts to persuade; it fails; he therefore proceeds to a plain statement of the alternatives, and demands decision of her as he is accustomed to demand it of himself: "Answer me tomorrow." Disciplined and effective thought is not usually the concomitant of slavery to the lusts of the body. The point is too obvious to need labouring; that Shakespeare did in fact grasp it, may be seen from the speech of Lucio in this play—the skimble-skamble disorganized stuff one might expect from a nature wasted by self-indulgence.

Angelo's consuetude with decisive thinking on ethical matters is nowhere so well revealed as in his reflections on himself when he realizes that he desires Isabel. The sequence of thought reveals the nature of the man, and is in itself so carefully thought out and vividly imagined, that one cannot in face of it deny that Shakespeare valued his creation here.

His very first concern is to apportion moral responsibility:

> What's this? What's this? Is this her fault, or
>   mine?

He settles his own problems as decisively as he settles the problems of others:

> Not she, nor doth she tempt, but it is I.

His next question is typical of the reflective moralist: it is an attempt to formulate new experience and to consider how far the personal discovery indicates a general truth:

> Can it be
> That modesty may more betray our sense
> Than woman's lightness?

and immediately after, to pronounce on the moral implications of the experience, to place it accurately in the moral scale:

> Having waste ground enough
> Shall we desire to raze the sanctuary
> And pitch our evils there? O fy, fy, fy!

Next—perhaps the greatest revelation of all —comes his immediate impulse to re-value his whole being in the light of new knowledge, re-estimating the old by the light of the new:

> What dost thou, or what art thou, Angelo?

Here is revealed—and Shakespeare cannot have done this with his eyes shut—Angelo's ability to state a problem correctly with rapid logic and moral simplicity: he is saying, in effect, "One of two conclusions may be drawn: either I am what I have always thought, in which case the problem is, How can I do this thing? or I am one to whom such a thing *is* natural, in which case the problem is, What evil nature is mine?" The pressure of an intellectual and spiritual agony forces that dilemma into the simple frame, "What dost thou, or what art thou, Angelo?" This is followed by as full a piece of self-knowledge as any Shakespearean hero ever showed:

> Dost thou desire her foully for those things
> That make her good?

The exhaustion that follows this simultaneous suffering and self-scrutiny reveals itself in the next words, which are a helpless longing to be rid of the whole problem:

> O let her brother live!
> Thieves for their robbery have authority,
> When judges steal themselves.

It is one of the great touches of this play that Shakespeare makes Angelo so desperate in his longing to escape the temptation of Isabel's presence, that he is willing to abandon the position for which he contended in the argument with Escalus; faced with the alternative of betraying his conception of justice or enduring again the compelling presence of Isabel, he weakens so far as to use almost the very instance that he had before dismissed as irrelevant. It is not sufficiently recognized that to Angelo the betrayal of his trust as a servant of justice was as grave a matter as unchastity was to Isabel, and the weakening on this point is evidence of the irresistible force of the temptation that Isabel put in his path. (It has been shown, earlier in the play, that the presence of Isabel was such as to silence and captivate even Lucio, the most inveterate brothel-haunter and brothel-flaunter of them all.) And Angelo's next words show how swiftly the temptation had prevailed, for they reveal that he had (immediately after the thought of avoiding her) felt in prospect the pang of *not* seeing her again:

> What! do I love her,
> That I desire to hear her speak again,
> And feast upon her eyes?

There is more in this than the mere lust of the body, and in one sense Angelo, in his bid for Isabel, is an object of pity as well as horror. What he feels for her is love—a love begun by the recognition of a complementary mind ("she speaks, and 'tis such sense, that my sense breeds with it"), confirmed by the sympathy of one disciplined and virtuous nature for another, and mounting to the inexplicable catalysis of love where the body too is desired, both for itself and as a means to participation in the soul. Isabel's soul is by the nature of her vocation beyond his reach—at least, her soul in the fair state which attracted his, for bodily possession must inevitably have been accompanied by the defacing of the essence that first drew him and so would have been, at best, the expense of spirit in a waste of shame. Something of this tragic impasse is in the concluding passage of this soliloquy:

> O cunning enemy, that to catch a saint
> With saints doth bait thy hook! Most dangerous
> Is that temptation, that doth goad us on
> To sin in loving virtue.

That this *is* the concluding passage is surely remarkable: that only now, after the sequence of reflection, Angelo finds a place to remark the severity of his fate. He does

but remark it; there is not the outcry that a tragedy would have found scope for. The situation of Angelo is, as it were, a diagram of a tragedy; all the lines of the structure are clearly drawn, but because this is a comedy, the mass and weight are not insisted on; they can, nevertheless, be experienced by imaginative reconstruction.

Shakespeare has here performed an extraordinary artistic feat. He has assured us by external witness (the Duke) that Angelo has spent years in the pursuit of self-knowledge and self-discipline; he had substantiated this by giving Angelo a style of speech that reflects such mental habits; he has in this soliloquy shown "the thing itself": the very process of self-awareness in the moment of becoming conscious; he has placed a man of this kind in a situation that overthrows him and in which he knows himself overthrown. Yet all this is managed within the frame of comedy, because it is indicated only and is not given full tragic dimensions; the emphasis is on the intellectual diagram, not on the emotional impact.

In Angelo's next soliloquy, Shakespeare combines restraint with lucidity in such a way that the personal agony is held in solution without being precipitated, yet the nature of the precipitation can be known, if one cares to enter into an imaginative experiencing of Angelo's description of his state. It is, when thought upon, the state of a man in hell. Nor Brutus nor Macbeth ever endured such spiritual agony before the commission of a crime. In this soliloquy the extreme of anguish is reached, for in it the will to God and the will to evil do not so much struggle, as co-exist in mutual loathing, while Angelo experiences the external antipathy of these adversaries. For he still prays. The tension of his divided will is in the very make of his first words:

> When I would pray and think, I think and pray
> To several subjects.

The phrases themselves are back to back, straining in opposed directions. In the whole speech we see the man re-living the failure of his attempted meditations— their failure in every stage, for the traditional stages of meditation are all referred to. First, recollection, the putting oneself by a deliberate act of the will in the frame of mind to attend, in thought and prayer, to God; secondly, the words of preparatory prayers; thirdly, "invention," that is, the presentation to oneself of a vivid image of the subject of meditation; finally, the bringing into play of the affections. Angelo has failed in every stage: he cannot exert his will to the point of recollection, his words are empty, his imagination fails to hold God before his eyes and "anchors on Isabel," and in his affections there is, not God, but the "strong and swelling evil" of his conception. In despair of meditation he has turned to study; this too has failed. Mere self-respect, the last strong-point, has dispersed, and his attitude to himself, now, is as chaotic as his attitude to good and evil. The old things seem false, disparate, and vacuous, the new consciousness of "blood" (the passions he had dismissed as negligible) is foreign and incorrigibly strong. The last two lines of the speech:

Let's write good angel on the devil's horn,
'Tis not the devil's crest

sum up what he has learned from his reflections on his life and this sudden new light on it: he had writ himself good angel, only to find that the devil within remained, and proved the superscription wrong.

The realization in dramatic terms of a crucial state of mind and soul, which follows this, is one of the finest things in Shakespeare. Angelo's will is temporarily paralysed: it cannot direct him to either of the opposed alternatives, since both are desired at once. And the confusion of his faculties is the more severe since both are also hated at once. In the physical images he uses to refer to his attitudes to good and evil, there is nausea—both against evil ("the strong and swelling evil of my conception") and against good ("Heaven in

my mouth, as if I did but only chew his name"). But the rigour of life is that one must act even when unable to decide— emergent occasions do not wait on precedent devotions—and to Angelo thus paralysed there enters, for the second time, Isabel. He is thrown into an indescribable excitement and desperation, so extreme as to seem to him insupportable:

Why does my blood thus muster to my heart,
Making both it unable for itself,
And dispossessing all my other parts
Of necessary fitness?
So play the foolish throngs with him that swounds;
Come all to help him, and so stop the air
By which he should revive.

The metaphor is imaginative in Coleridge's sense: it is at all points germane to the feeling it describes (the press and thickening of desire, the curious flocking expectations of it, the faintness of body and suspension of the autonomy of the spirit). So too is the metaphor to which this gives place when (as we may assume) Isabel actually appears; the quality of the words "obsequious fondness" and "untaught love" suggests with all imaginable delicacy the throng of irrepressible tender impulses as he sees her. The element of tender affection in Angelo's response to the physical presence of Isabel is merely suggested, but it is there; Shakespeare *saw* Angelo as humanly complex, but he has not *demanded* our attention to the whole of the complexity.

The scene which follows is one difficult to understand if the nature and the predicament of Angelo have not been properly grasped. This scene shows Angelo's will moving, in action, to one of its two poles; this it must show, for it is only in the passion of the spirit that irreconcilables can co-exist. They struggle confusedly for existence in the first few interchanges of Angelo with Isabel, where one speech flatly contradicts another. With consummate truth to the reality of a state of extreme indecision, Shakespeare has shown that the deciding

element in the contention is Angelo's recoil
from whichever alternative is uppermost
in his mind. Isabel pleads that he should
countenance Claudio's fault and he recoils
at once from his own:

Ha! fie, these filthy vices!

In exactly the same way, when Isabel points
him to the alternative, by insisting on the
overriding importance of the soul, he recoils now from this and presses to the other
pole of his will:

Might there not be a charity in sin
To save this brother's life?

When Isabel, misunderstanding him, replies,

It is no sin at all, but charity

he recoils again and corrects her:

Pleas'd you to do't, at peril of your soul,
Were equal poise of sin and charity.

It is when Isabel flatly refuses him and denounces the yielding of the body as
"shame," that he as decisively commits
himself to the other extreme. The balance
is now struck, and Angelo who so far has
hardly known whether he argues with Isabel, or with himself, or whether he is in
fact feeling his way to the beginning of the
seduction in the only way he knows, now
enters the struggle with Isabel and puts
into it all the pent-up strength of will that
recently in the struggle with himself could
find no direction for its power. The veer-
ings from pole to pole now cease, and the
whole momentum of a powerful nature, of
a will accustomed to browbeat the opposition of the subordinate faculties, of a temper inflexible in decision and rapid in action, flares up to the fuel of this occasion
and consumes Isabel. There is the exulta-
tion of release as well as the savagery of a
desire which is the obverse of love, in Angelo's words:

I have begun;
And now I give my sensual race the rein:
Fit thy consent to my sharp appetite;

Lay by all nicety and prolixious blushes,
That banish what they sue for; redeem thy
  brother
By yielding up thy body to my will,
Or else he must not only die the death
But thy unkindness shall his death draw out
To lingering sufferance: answer me tomorrow.

Angelo's passion of cruelty is as extreme
as the suffering that gave it birth, and it is
in his enormities that we see fully what had
been the pitch of his agony before; just as
in Isabel's rounding on Claudio we see reflected the precedent anguish of her alternatives. This cruelty is further exacerbated
by the hell of lusting after the body where
primarily the soul is loved.

There are masterly touches in this scene,
touches which cannot but be missed if one
blinds oneself with the assumption that
Angelo is narrow-souled and that Shakespeare's attitude to his type was one of merciless exposure. It is, for instance, impossible for the unsympathetic critic to value
aright those interchanges where Angelo
says plainly that Claudio shall not die if
Isabel give him love, and, because Isabel is
unwilling to believe he can be in earnest,
has to reiterate it. His words

Believe me, on mine honour,
My words express my purpose

spring from Angelo as he has formerly
seen himself, one whose word is his bond,
and he has forgotten that in this new situation there is no reason why Isabel should
value it. This is fine, but what follows is
finer still. Isabel rounds on him:

Little honour to be much believ'd!

and threatens to proclaim his villainy.
Angelo's response,

Who will believe thee, Isabel?

is nothing less than tenderness, a kind of
compassion for her predicament, in the
midst of tyranny. It is momentary; the use
of "thee" gives place at once to "you" in
the next three lines where mentally he sees
her opposing him before the eyes of the

world; then it recurs when he prescribes the manner of her consent and anticipates their intimacy. Then again, at the end of the speech, when he repeats that it is impossible her denunciation should be believed, "thee" gives place again, in the final abandonment to conscious cruelty, to "you":

> As for you,
> Say what you can, my false o'er weighs your true.

The subsequent deepening of his villainy, the rapid blunting of a soul once its first fine edge is lost, has its parallel in Macbeth, and no more casts doubt on the validity of Angelo's first estate than does Macbeth's blood-boltered villainy make his earlier scruples incredible.

"Dull to all proceedings," he fights to maintain all that is left to him, the "credent bulk" of a public esteem which has become a mockery to him.[4]

So R. W. Chambers has written and has also said of Angelo's prayer to be put out of his misery (in the final reckoning with the Duke):

Surely it is concerning repentance like this that it is written, "There is joy in the presence of the angels of God." [5]

This Angelo of Shakespeare's has been too little regarded. In consequence, the harmony of the play has been untuned, the great antithesis of justice and mercy reduced to a shadow of itself, and the complexity of Angelo's character and experience passed over.

It may be that Angelo's breaking-off of the nuptials with Mariana is the mote that has loomed large to the critical eye. But Angelo is not plot-proof; the connection with Mariana is essential to the untying of the dramatic knot; Angelo is not the first of Shakespeare's characters to bestride the

narrow world of tidy dénouements like a Colossus, and Shakespeare may have thought, if he gave it a thought at all, that there is no real matter for surprise in the fact that a man whose blood was very snow-broth should have broken off the negotiations for a marriage of convenience which had ceased to offer the conveniences for whose sake it was first contemplated. The delineation of Angelo's character in the scenes that come before we have learned anything of the Mariana business is so passionately done, so consistent in every detail, so speaking a likeness of scrupulous integrity, that it is Mariana who must square with this, not this with Mariana.

It is possible to regard *Measure for Measure* as an experiment by Shakespeare: an attempt to handle, in a comedy, a character comparable to the characters of the tragedies. It is even possible that the hesitations in the critical attitude to Angelo are in some measure due to the failure to see this—a failure born of the practice of looking for tragic intensity only in those characters who are by their whole nature tragically incompatible with their circumstances. Angelo, like any ordinary character in a comedy, is made to see himself in a new light by the impact of an external accident—in his case, the accident of meeting Isabel. But, unlike the ordinary characters of comedy, he bears the marks of having been imagined intensely in all his complexity and capacity for suffering, just as Shakespeare's tragic characters are imagined, though his suffering is not fully bodied forth. It may be this departure from practice that has crippled the criticism of *Measure for Measure*. The hypothesis is strengthened by a similar phenomenon in the criticism of *The Winter's Tale*. Leontes' jealousy is not native to him, if we are to believe in the Leontes of the later part of the play—it is an excrescence on his nature, which the course of events removes—and Leontes too suffers from his own passions with an intensity more familiar in

---

[4] R. W. Chambers, *The Jacobean Shakespeare and "Measure for Measure,"* p. 46.
[5] Ibid. p. 46.

the tragic frame. And Leontes has produced the same outcry and recoil in those who would interpret the play, and that outcry in turn has led to a neglect of the human complexity and intensity with which Shakespeare has endowed him.

Whatever the cause of the slighting of Angelo, it is time it be made good, time for critics of Shakespeare's art to accept, in Angelo, yet another attempt to carry human understanding as far as it may reach.

For of Angelo one may say, as Professor Alexander has said of Macbeth:

Shakespeare unfolds the crime in a manner that would satisfy Rhadamanthus himself, yet brings home to us the truth in Donne's Christian surmise: "Thou knowest this man's fall, but thou knowest not his wrastling; which perchance was such that almost his very fall is justified and accepted of God." [6]

[6] P. Alexander, *Shakespeare's Life and Art,* p. 173.

Arthur Sewell

The Character of Angelo

THERE is a general agreement that in Shakespeare's tragedies we witness a process of "chemical change" in the hero's spirit, brought about by a situation which makes demands upon him which he cannot fulfil and by a moral failure which has its issue at last in a reorganization of his whole being. Character-change and character-development, at any rate, are fundamental elements in Shakespeare's great tragic dramas. He was not only concerned with what happens to a man; he was also concerned with what happens within a man. The nature of this change and development is crucial in an understanding of the relation between Shakespeare's vision and his creation of the tragic characters.

Before I discuss that, however, it seems to me useful to consider the nature of "change" in certain other characters created in another mode.

In *The Winter's Tale* and *The Tempest* the characters of Leontes, Alonzo, and Sebastian undergo what certainly appears to be character-development, going hand in hand with repentance and reconciliation at the end of the play. Leontes, having learned the truth, repents immediately, but has to wait sixteen years for reconciliation. Alonzo and Sebastian are taught a brief but bitter lesson by Prospero. We would say, in everyday language, that they become changed men, and it is part of the optimism of tragi-comic effect that we should suppose the change to be lasting. The motivation of the change, and the evidence for its probable permanence, do not seem to be wholly adequate and are, at least, mainly mechanical. How mechanical it is we may illustrate perhaps from the extreme case of Iachimo. The inner transformation (if we suppose there to be one) is only conveniently brought about: in Leontes by the words of the oracle declaring Hermione to be chaste, and in Alonzo and Sebastian by the discomforts and distresses which Prospero imposes upon them. Attitude before and attitude after are really opaque to each other, although they are credibly represented as belonging to the one character. Personality is not reorganized but metamorphosed. We recognize the new address to life, the change in mental attitude, but Shakespeare has been little concerned (Alonzo and Sebastian are, of course, minor characters) to explore and justify those deeper processes by which this change might have been brought about.

Why, then, are we convinced by the change—or, at least, why do we accept it?

For two reasons, I think. In the first place, these characters change in a manner directly and unambiguously derived from the comprehensive (and ultimately optimistic) vision of the play. In the play's magnetic field, as it were, we do not doubt that all the characters will be drawn towards the pole. Just as character itself may be directly determined by the moral vision of the play, so also in the same way what happens to character and within character may be so determined and made credible. Secondly, the change in character is one which we approve and which agrees with the social judgement. It is a return to what is more desirable by way of nature; for in the Romances evil in man is an accident and not the original condition of his being. Repentance and forgiveness, after all, con-

Reprinted from *Character and Society in Shakespeare* (Oxford, 1951), pp. 64–72, by permission of the Clarendon Press. Title supplied by the present editor.

serve order and harmony in society. Such changes need no deeper motivation than the persuasion of external events. If a man is punished, we grant that he will do better in future. If a man is undeceived, we grant that he will not persist in folly. It is the assumption of comedy that men and women are capable of being educated, and in comedy the Law (as it were) is often a schoolmaster to bring men to their senses. At least, as with Lucio in *Measure for Measure*, they can be restrained. We do not, then, in characters such as these discover any real change. We discover rather a change of attitude, the result not of any inner motivation but of the teaching of external events. In something the same way, we might say, Elizabeth Bennet loses her prejudice, and Darcy forgets his pride; marriage (we believe) will see to it that there is no backsliding. What the readers, what the audience, *want* to believe, determines what is, in fact, credible.

Even more illuminating than the treatment of the characters just mentioned from the Romances is the treatment of the character of Angelo in *Measure for Measure*. He, too, undergoes changes, and changes of a very dramatic kind; and he has always been something of a puzzle to the critics. It is possible that the groundlings saw Angelo as a mere hypocrite, who sent them back to their viciousness with the comfortable feeling that the seeming best of men have the itch as much as they. But it is quite clear that Shakespeare intended something more serious than that. It is also possible to see in Angelo the study of a man whose appetites have been too tightly reined, and who is overwhelmed by a "fetichistic" lust for a girl who comes in the robes of the nunnery to plead for her brother's life. And we can begin with this view in our attempt to relate the study of Angelo to the general vision of the play. For Angelo must be what the vision of the play makes of him. If, for example, the play is, as R. W. Chambers suggested, a

study in penitence and punishment, and if it ends with the "stuff of Christianity," the idea of redemption, then the psychological study of this "fetichistic lust" must be auxiliary to a study of the moral nature of man. If Angelo is to be seen in the end as fallen man redeemed, Shakespeare's study of him must be the study of a human soul.

One preliminary comment is necessary. What may be held (if anything at all) to be unsatisfactory or incomplete in the study of Angelo has been explained and excused by the fact that he is by no means the central figure of the play, and consequently a certain morbidity may be allowed in his character—as though what is morbid, though shading into the "normal," may properly be part of the periphery of attention. One may suppose, that is to say, that a pathological study, when it is not the heart and centre of the play, may nevertheless be properly introduced into the play, since the moral has to do with the pathological, and who shall say where the one becomes the other? Angelo's case, had it been the centre of the play, would have been morbid, because it is not universal. Since it is not the centre, so the argument runs, it serves to darken and deepen the universality of the play, and has, as it were by derivation, a secondary, a derived universality.

If this is so, however, criticism must not load the morbidity with more significance than it can bear. It must not say: The play is about "redemption," therefore Angelo is redeemed, *and* therefore his conduct can only have such-and-such an interpretation. Criticism, having decided that the theme of the play is a study in "penitence and punishment," must not read into the character a psychological subtlety and a moral understanding which could only have been there if that character had been a central character in the play. Criticism must not proceed on the lines of the hypothesis— Now what should I have had to say of this character had he been the central character of the play? And this is precisely what Mr.

J. I. M. Stewart, in his concern to defend Shakespeare against Dr. Bridges, does when he writes: "In the last act of the play [Angelo] is like a man fighting his way through a dream, loaded with the awful consciousness of having done irreparable ill." This judgement might apply to Macbeth, but not to Angelo. For the last act of the play in no way bears this out, as I shall shortly have occasion to show. The truth is that such words as Mr. Stewart uses ought only to be used about a central character whose "awful consciousness" has indeed been the central study of the play.

We learn enough about Angelo, even though he is not the central character, to know that he is involved in the most awful moral crisis of the play; a moral crisis in which might well have been represented the universal crisis of man, in which there might have been a particular exposure of man's fall from grace. Indeed, the main responsibility for representing this case of man is laid on Angelo; but Angelo cannot properly represent it, just because he is not the central character of the play.

Nor is it at all the concern of *Measure for Measure* to make such a study of "awful consciousness." The world of the play is not really the world of human souls. It is true that in the last act there is some play with the notions of penitence and forgiveness; the Law is threatened and then remitted. But the play is called *Measure for Measure*, and the deeper seriousness of penitence and forgiveness are uneasily accommodated in the treatment of such a theme. The final concern of the play is not with redemption or with grace but with the Law, and when the Law seems at the end of the play to be abrogated it is surely an error to suppose that its place has been taken by a covenant of grace. For the Law, in fact, is not abrogated. The marriages imposed—Angelo's as much as Lucio's—are salutary, not blessed. This so-called forgiveness, this remission of the Law, is in some ways more terrible than the rigour of the law suspended; for it implies that lust may, after all, be bridled as well by marriage as by death. Angelo's marriage is not very different from Lucio's; it is not, surely, the marriage of a man who has undergone a "saving experience." It is a marriage which will conserve (and perhaps continuate) the society to which both Angelo and Lucio belong.

No world of evil makes a bid in *Measure for Measure* for the soul of a man, for such a world always both is and is not the creation of man. The lust that overwhelms Angelo seems to spring, psychologically, from within, but in a truer sense it overwhelms him from without. It does not come to him as a revelation of himself, as Macbeth's ambitious purpose both surprises and convicts him and makes him tremble as at a revelation of himself. There is always a separateness between Angelo and his lust; and the lust is simple and opaque, except after psychological analysis, to the earlier nature of the man. Angelo's lust has no more poetry in it than rape in a court of law; and had he indeed belonged to the world of human souls the lust would have been pitifully, terribly, in the poetry. And so in Angelo, changed and remorseful, what was this lust, never having been other than separate from him, can only be destroyed. In a human soul all may be transformed, but nothing destroyed.

Nevertheless, the implied agony and the moral seriousness of Angelo's case are such that they cannot be sustained unless he is seen—unless in Shakespeare's vision he has been apprehended—as a human soul. For we refuse to accept him either as a study in morbid psychology or as a canting hypocrite. We must conclude, then, that in Angelo Shakespeare has introduced a situation, a case, and a character, intractable to the working out of the comprehensive vision of the play. And this is as much as to say that the vision itself is uncertain, for vision seeks to discover itself in character.

In Angelo, vision does not so discover itself, and it is instructive to note in what manner and measure it fails. The imagery in which Angelo expresses himself scarcely ever reveals the darker recesses of his being; nothing rises from the centre. The promptings of his lust express themselves in external figures, in the very language of the Law, and the appetite has no status or activity in the world of the spirit. Once recognized, it turns outward to explain itself, using language which takes its substance and its currency from secular society.

> O heavens!
> Why does my blood thus muster to my heart,
> Making both it unable for itself,
> And dispossessing all my other parts
> Of necessary fitness?

Then, immediately, Angelo turns to a mere simile, a memory from social experience, elaborating but not enriching, not generating the emotion:

> So play the foolish throngs with one that swounds;
> Come all to help him, and so stop the air
> At which he would revive.

This is not the appetite speaking, but the man about the appetite. So, later, lust takes its language from the Law, and loses thereby its nature, since it takes this language and leaves it untransformed. It speaks of "accusation," "calumnies," "seeing," "banishment," and "lingering sufferance." Even after the satisfaction, Angelo does not see the evil he has done except in these terms of Law and reputation—and some doubts about his own safety:

> This deed unshapes me quite, makes me unpregnant
> And dull to all proceedings. A deflower'd maid,
> And by an eminent body that enforc'd
> The Law against it! But that her tender shame
> Will not proclaim against her maiden loss,
> How might she tongue me! Yet reason dares her no;
> For my authority bears so credent bulk,
> That no particular scandal once can touch;
> But it confounds the breather.

There is no penitence here; there is no exhaustion of lustful appetite; the lawyer is talking about the lecher. It is not for nothing that at the end of the last Act the Duke says, when Claudio is known to be still alive:

> By this, Lord Angelo perceives he's safe:
> Methinks I see a quickening in his eye.

The Duke speaks here of a man not redeemed but reprieved. But there is something in Angelo's case, and in the treatment of that case, which would make us wish him both redeemed and reprieved.

William Empson

Sense in *Measure for Measure*

THERE are only about ten uses of the word [*sense*] in the play, but I think almost all of them carry forward a puzzle which is essential to its thought. It is not denied that the word then covered (1) "sensuality" and (2) "sensibility," and I maintain that it also covered (3) "sensibleness," though in a less direct way, through the ideas of "a truth-giving feeling" and "a reasonable meaning." Clearly the equations between these three could carry very relevant ironies, though the effect is not so much a covert assertion as something best translated into questions. Are Puritans hard? (Is not-one not-two?) Are they liable to have crazy outbreaks? (Is not-one not-three?) Is mere justice enough? (Is three two?) To be sure, these questions look very unlike the flat false identity of one idea with another, but I think the state of the word then made them easier to impose. It seems to have been neither analysed nor taken as simple; it points directly into the situation where it is used, implying a background of ideas which can be applied to the situation, but somehow as if the word itself did not name them; it is a shorthand term, rather than a solid word in which two of the meanings can be equated. And yet, as the play works itself out, there is a sort of examination of the word as a whole, of all that it covers in the cases where it can be used rightly; or rather an examination of sanity itself, which is seen crumbling and dissolving in the soliloquies of Angelo.

No doubt, in any case, the play is not fully satisfactory, and it has been argued that the suggestions of extra meaning are merely the result of Shakespeare doing the best he can with a bad plot. Mr. R. W. Chambers, in *Man's Unconquerable Mind*, seemed to feel that the Bard had been unfairly insulted by modernistic persons, and urged truly enough that he made the plot less disagreeable than he found it. But no one, I take it, maintains that Shakespeare set out to write an attack on virginity (or for that matter on James I, if he is the Duke). The rebuttal does not come close enough to the idea in question; nor, I think, does Mr. Dover Wilson's gallant and romantic defence of Prince Hal, or Dr. Tillyard's patient and illuminating collection of evidence that the scheme of the Shakespeare History plays was drawn from a pompous contemporary myth made up to flatter the Tudors (a thing which he seems to admire more than it deserves). Nobody has denied that the Histories build up the Tudors, or that Prince Hal was meant to be a popular success. What has occasionally crossed the minds of critics, for quite a long time now, is to wonder what Shakespeare thought about it, and whether he cannot sometimes be found grumbling to himself about the plots that he was using, in a way that the audience was not expected to notice. No doubt this puts the contrast rather too strongly. I think a certain double attitude to Prince Hal is meant to be made public; indeed the idea that he could not be both a reliable friend and a popular hero is a very straightforward "moral," even if not a prominent one. But in any case the question how many of the audience noticed the two levels of meaning does not seem to me crucial. As the evidence about the Elizabethan mind piles up, we are tacitly asked

Reprinted from *The Structure of Complex Words* (London, 1951), pp. 270–84. All rights reserved.
Used by permission of New Directions.

to believe that Shakespeare could not possibly have disagreed with it, or have dared to show that he disagreed. I think he was a more self-indulgent kind of man than that, as well as not such a stupid one. Of course the plot had to be something that would go down, but when he came to write the thing (pretty fast) the characters had to say what he could imagine for them. *Measure for Measure* is I think one of the most striking cases where the feelings in his words jib at a wholehearted acceptance of the story, without being planned as a secret meaning for the wiser few or even marking a clear-cut opinion in the author. Perhaps I am making too much fuss about adopting this common-place point of view, but the idea seems to have been much blown upon lately by historical-minded critics, and yet I cannot see that they have brought any evidence against it.

However, the recent drift of various British critics towards royalism is mild compared to that of various American ones towards behaviourism, which happens to go in the same direction. At least I imagine that that cult, so powerful in linguistics, is the ultimate reason why so many American critics of Shakespeare claim that their work is "objective." If we give *objective* its full claims, to "wonder what Shakespeare thought about it" becomes a disgraceful self-indulgence; a critic should limit himself to rigid proofs, like the scientist that he is. That is, in effect, he should talk about the author as one of a type, not as an individual acquaintance; to a certain extent this really gets done, and it seems clear to me that the method produces superficial criticism. No doubt the timidity of the thing saves a critic from the more flamboyant errors of the last century; and you may reasonably say that we cannot make Shakespeare into a personal acquaintance. But it is enough to refute the behaviourist, on this issue, if he admits that we can make *anybody* into a personal acquaintance; that we can ever get any "insight" into another person's feelings. One of the

things a critic has normally claimed to do is to show this sort of insight about authors; there is nothing that I can see in the theory of behaviourism, only in its "atmosphere," to get this forbidden; and if a critic insists that he has no such insight, it seems to me, he is only saying in an unnecessarily pompous manner (and sometimes quite falsely) that he is unfit to do his work.

I shall assume then, in the old-fashioned way, that the first thing to consider about *Measure for Measure* is why Shakespeare was interested in the story; because this interest is what will cause any drag there may be against the obvious theatrical values of the characters. We are to imagine him coming across it in the Italian, perhaps translated offhand, of Cinthio's collection of 1565, which he was already using for the plot of *Othello*, and then looking up Whetstone's dramatization of it (1578) for some extra tips. It was a clumsy plot, needing a good deal of tinkering, but it would carry a part of what was on his mind. This was very complex. There was a strand of loathing for sexuality in any form, partly no doubt as an intellectual agreement with the Puritans, but one that he recognises as a diseased frame of mind; and contrasting with this a loathing for the cruelty which this line of feeling produced in Puritans, above all for the claim that to indulge the cruelty satisfies justice. The contrast was one with many ramifications, and my own guess is that he saw the wicked deputy as one of the Cold People of Sonnet 94, the lilies that fester and smell worse than weeds; he christened him Angel; after that he found the plot interesting. He was not in the mood to write comedies, and the old real situation of the Sonnets, however irrelevant, was a source of energy. The first speech describing Angelo is a series of reminiscences from the Sonnets, and after that he develops on his own. I think that a use of *sense* in Sonnet 35 helps to show why the word became a crux of the play.

No more be griev'd at that which thou hast
  done,
Roses have thorns, and silver fountains mud,
Clouds and eclipses stain both Moon and Sun,
And loathsome canker lives in sweetest bud.
All men make faults, and even I in this,
Authorising thy trespass with compare,
Myself corrupting salving thy amiss,
Excusing thy sins more than thy sins are:
For to thy sensual fault I bring in sense,
Thy adverse party is thy Advocate,
And gainst myself a lawful plea commence,
Such civil war is in my love and hate,
    That I an accessary needs must be,
    To that sweet thief which sourly robs from
    me.

"I bring in reason, arguments to justify it" or "I bring in feelings about it, feel it more important than it really was (and therefore excuse it more than it needs)" or "I bring extra sensuality to it; I enjoy thinking about it and making arguments to defend it, so that my sensuality sympathises with yours." Sensuality is the predicate, I think. In any case the subtle confusion of the word is used for a mood of fretted and exhausting casuistry; the corruption of the best makes it the worst; charity is good, but has strange and shameful roots; the idea of a lawsuit about such matters is itself shameful, and indeed more corrupt than the natural evil. If he associated the word with this passage it would carry most of the atmosphere of *Measure for Measure*.

The first use of the word in the play is by the gay Lucio, when he goes to Isabella at her nunnery to tell her about the pregnancy and ask her to beg for her brother's life. (To avoid obscurity I shall summarise the plot here and there in brackets. Angelo, left in command of the dukedom, has revived an old law imposing death for sex outside marriage, and this falls on Claudio though he is already betrothed and prepared to marry.) It is hard to get clear about Elizabethan politeness, but I take it Lucio is a bit muddled though still casual. He wants to respect her highmindedness, but he has to treat the scandal as trivial to induce her to help, so he falls into a verbose style which the bitter woman thinks is mocking her virtue.

> A man whose blood
> Is very snow-broth: one who never feels
> The wanton stings and motions of the sense;
> But doth rebate, and blunt his natural edge
> With profits of the mind; Study, and fast. . . .
>   . . . hath pick'd out an act,
> Under whose heavy sense your brother's life
> Falls into forfeit: he arrests him on it. . . .
>   (i.4.57)

"Profits of the mind" with its Puritan commercialism makes an effort to get the nun's point of view, but "blunt your natural edge" is a phrase he would more naturally use (say) of making yourself stupid by heavy drinking. He clearly feels, though he cannot say outright, that Angelo's habits have cost him his "common sense." However we must guard against taking this as part of his intended meaning for *sense*; the meaning "sensuality" is very unequivocal. Indeed one might say that this clearcut use of the word is put first in the play to thrust the meaning "sensuality" on our attention and make us treat it as the dominant one. Yet the word acts as a sort of euphemism, and this suggestion is supported by the jauntiness of Lucio's whole tone. The form implies that sensuality is only one of the normal functions of the senses, and the rest of the speech implies that to neglect them is to become *blunted*, *heavy* (cruel) and so forth. Lucio does not want to annoy Isabella by saying this plainly, even by the relative plainness of a covert assertion; but it can hang about in his mind, and there is evidence that it does so when *sense* crops up again as the "meaning" or "intention" of the heavy Act. This sort of thing needs to be distinguished from asserting an equation, and indeed is prior to it. If you say that I am ascribing magical powers to Shakespeare in making him put all this into the speech of Lucio, the answer is that the word was hanging about in Shakespeare's mind in the same way.

The next use is an aside of Angelo when first fascinated by Isabella (he will bargain to give her her brother's life in exchange for her body).

> She speaks and 'tis
> Such sense, that my Sense breeds with it. Fare
> you well.   (ii.2.143)

Pope emended *breeds* to "bleeds," making him express pity only, which is quite off the point. It shows I think how obscure the Shakespearean structure of meaning in the word had become to the Augustans; because the meaning "sensuality" is obviously wanted here, if you can feel that it is linguistically possible. Angelo's first use of the word is "wise or reasonable meaning," and then the meaning "sensuality," which Lucio has made dominant for this stage of the play, pokes itself forward and is gratified by the second use of the word as a pun. Even in the second use I am not sure that "sensuality" can be called the chief meaning of the word; the suggestion of *breeds* is rather that both the "meanings in his mind" and his "sense-data" have sensuality growing inside them—added to them, so to speak, as an Implication. So I think one could class both uses as equations of Type I,[1] with sensuality acting as a dominant; however it is quite enough to feel that the word is given two simple meanings one after another. Presumably the capital letter when the word is repeated merely means that the actor should emphasize it to bring out the pun.

In real life it seems rather unlikely that this pun would occur to Angelo. It occurred to Shakespeare, and was wanted; to Lucio it could occur spontaneously, with a cheerful feeling that sensuality goes with sensibleness; but to Angelo the combination of meanings in the word can only appear as a hideous accident. The only touching side of Angelo is that he is genuinely astonished by his desires. (It is taken for granted that he could not make love to her

---

[1] A reference to one of the classes of ambiguity or complex meaning in Empson's system. For more detail, see the discussion of "statements in words," *Structure of Complex Words*, Ch. II.—Ed.

in the ordinary way, though there is nothing to prevent him.) Yet the real irony, apart from the verbal accident, is that her coldness, even her rationality, is what has excited him; the two things are patently connected as in the word, though not in his system of ideas. Possibly with his usual injustice he feels that what she has just said ("if *you* remember a natural guiltiness") is already a loose way of talking. It is curious in any case to remember the decision of the N.E.D. that the meaning "good judgement" for *sense* does not appear till the later half of the century; this passage is not using it alone, but gets all the effect of it.

In the next use, after the interview is over, Angelo is not thinking of the word as a pun, and indeed the possible connections have become so elaborate that the meanings are hard to tie down.

> What's this? What's this? is this her fault or
>   mine?
> The Tempter or the Tempted, who sins most?
> Not she: nor doth she tempt: but it is I
> That, lying by the violet in the Sun,
> Do as the Carrion does, not as the flower,
> Corrupt with virtuous season. Can it be,
> That Modesty may more betray our sense
> Than woman's lightness? . . .   (ii.2.163)

The Arden edition's note says, very properly, that *sense* here means "sensuality, desire,"; that of course is the most prominent idea in Angelo's mind. But the recent punning may easily be recalled, and the immediately preceding metaphor is not obvious. In any case, why is our sensuality betrayed by being excited and released? We may be betrayed, but why it? To be sure, the modest woman may make the sensuality show itself, betray its presence; but if you adopt this rather strained meaning for the phrase the word need not mean "sensuality" uniquely. What is betrayed is perhaps our general tendency, our "gist or drift." Or again she may trick our sensuality into wrong actions, but this implies that our sensuality is normally present and usually good; it is nearer to Lucio's attitude than to

Angelo's. Nor does this attitude feel the meanings of the word to be sharply opposed. Indeed I am begging a question when I translate one of the meanings as "sensuality," because that tends to imply that the sexual desire in question is of an evil kind, whereas *sense* in itself does not have to add this Emotion. In the play it seems to be added insistently, not only by Angelo but by the presence of Isabella at the first use of the word; but perhaps Angelo is trying to exorcise this Emotion by the picture of the violet. There is a parallel confusion to that of *sense*, I think, in *season;* indeed part of the strength of a ready-made puzzle like that of *sense* is that it can impose itself as pattern on neighbouring words. The Arden note gives "benign influence of summer" for *virtuous season*—the warmth rots the carrion but makes the flower sweet. This idea is certainly present and gives a tidy metaphor. But it would make Isabella the sun, whereas she is clearly the modest violet, which he is lying by. If the sun is the natural strength which causes sexual desire, that itself can be good, the metaphor will imply. But if the violet is giving the *season,* the idea seems to be the smell of it, like *"seasoning"* in food, pepper for instance. Unlike the public and clear sunlight, this brings in ideas of privacy and of exciting the senses. He is no longer sure what the natural process can be, to which he contrasts himself, and has gone far towards accepting the confusion of meanings as a single and "profound" one, as in Type IV. I hope I have also shown that "sensuality" can still be regarded as a dominant, appearing only in the predicate as for Type I; and of course the passage is fully intelligible if you take "sensuality" as the only meaning of the word. In general I have not worried about the possible use of a deliberate ambiguity of equation structure, but when a character is actually puzzling about a word it is not surprising that the author should leave one open.

The next use of the word is in his second interview with Isabella.

ANG.:   Nay, but hear me,
Your sense pursues not mine; either you are ignorant,
Or seem so craftily; and that's not good.
                                                    (ii.4.73)

The pathetic or disgusting assumption of superior morality, in this rebuke to her for not understanding the bargain, finds an echo in the stock pun. Her meaning does not follow his, and also her desires do not start running when his do—that's not good; a girl ought to be docile. The Folio punctuation implies that ignorance would be bad as well as craft. "Now I give my sensual race the rein" he says soon after (ii.4.160); he is the only person in the play to use the adjective, and it is felt to go with a split in the meanings of *sense*, which should be harmoniously combined. In "your sense pursues not mine" the immediate context very definitely imposes "interpretation" ("the sense you put on my words") as the chief meaning, indeed to suppose it means "sensuality" is a satire on Angelo; but by this time it is so strong a dominant meaning that it arises easily.

There is a long pause before the next use of the word; Angelo has now settled down into crime, and can combine the meanings harmoniously enough in a way of his own.

> He should have lived
> Save that his riotous youth with dangerous sense
> Might in the times to come have ta'en revenge
> By so receiving a dishonour'd life
> With ransome of such shame.   (iv.4.8)

It is still with superior morality that he looks back on the most repulsive of his supposed actions. (Claudio begged Isabella to pay the price of his life, and she wished him dead for it. The Duke arranged that Angelo had Mariana instead, but no man in an Elizabethan play can tell one woman from another in the dark, and Angelo believes that he has killed Claudio after taking the price for saving him.) The *danger* of keeping the bargain and letting Claudio live would be that he would feel too deeply about it; *sense* covers "sensibility" here. But the reason why he is sure to have a keen sense of honour is that he is *riotous,* he is "sensual," for that either shows that you have strong feelings or develops them. In either case Angelo despises him for it; he is himself one of the cold people. The idea "meaning, purpose" is still possible in the word, but it is unimportant beside this startling irony.

There is no need to make these interpretations rigid, especially in so fluid a word. The simple view of the uses by Angelo is that he always means "sensuality" when in soliloquy and always pretends to mean something else when talking to other people. But this corresponds to the view of him as a hypocrite and villain all through; if you take the character as capable of struggle and development you need to suppose that his language carries the marks of it. At first he felt it as abnormal that the dominant meaning should emerge at all. In this example one does not need to invoke the idea of a "dominant meaning," because Angelo is explicit enough to make the immediate context impose both the meanings required; *riotous* gives "sensuality" and *dangerous* (to Angelo) gives "sensibility." *Riotous* is said first; to be sure, it is further away than *dangerous,* but it would be rather absurd to call this a less immediate context. I think "sensuality" is the idea that comes first in his mind, and acts as chief meaning of the word; if you had to choose only one meaning, what the logic of the passage requires is "sensibility," but it is regarded as a consequence. This is the order of the terms in the equation; the idea is "sensuality entails sensibility." He seems indeed to have moved the idea "sensuality" from being an intrusive dominant to being what he considers the head meaning of the word. He has no more to say with it, and does not use it again; the main force of its irony now turns against Isabella, and "sensuality," till now so prominent, becomes only a solemn paradox making a darkness in the background.

DUKE: Away with her; poor soul
She speaks this in th'infirmity of sense.
(v.1.47)

(Isabella is appealing against Angelo to the Duke at the gates of the city.) The use is simple enough, but the Duke is teasing Angelo, and a double meaning would be in order. He could hint at such ideas as "in the disorder of strong feeling—she has much to make her excited" or "in the weakness of mere reason and truth, which are inherently feeble beside the public monsters of hypocrisy and law." I think it is possible that the voice of Shakespeare behind him is preparing an irony of another kind. The Duke is still toying with the word a few lines later:

By mine honesty,
If she be mad, as I believe no other,
Her madness hath the oddest frame of sense,
Such a dependency of thing on thing,
As ere I heard in madness. (v.1.59)

If she has reason it is of a queer kind, not common sense but the obscure wisdom that Shakespeare expected in clowns and the half-mad. It is true that she would put an odd construction on *sense* (give it an odd *frame*); she is too other-worldly to use it in the common way. There is no pressure behind the passage, but I think it adds to the cumulative effect. Then Mariana has a use, important because free from irony; and her rhetoric (it is like that of Troilus) gives the word a fine chance to spread the peacock tail of its meanings. She has the shame of begging in public to be married to Angelo, who deserted her because she lost her money.

Noble Prince,
As there comes light from heaven, and words from breath,
As there is sense in truth, and truth in virtue,
I am affianced this man's wife, as strongly
As words could make up vows: And my good Lord,
But Tuesday night last gone, in's garden house,
He knew me as a wife. (v.1.223)

There is meaning in a true statement; there is purpose in making one; it is wise to tell the truth frankly. But the series goes from *sense* to *virtue*, and this tends to call out another part of the word's range. The kind of truth that is in virtue seems rather to be constancy or correspondence to natural law. Desire or passion, sensuality or sensibility, may make her constant; and she can decently assert them both in public; to be constant is to have the common sense of our normal feelings. The meanings are not merely compatible but undivided here; this is what the whole word is meant to do.

The next and final use raises a question about what Shakespeare himself thought of the play. Isabella still believes that Angelo has murdered her brother, and Mariana begs her for his life.

> MARI.:   Sweet Isabell, take my part:
> Lend me your knees, and all my life to come,
> I'll lend you all my life to do you service.
> DUKE: Against all sense you do importune
> her:
> Should she kneel down, in mercy of this fact,
> Her Brother's ghost, his paved bed would break,
> And take her hence in horror.   (v.1.433)

In the Duke's earlier plotting with Isabella, the chief impulse he appeals to in her is the desire to be revenged on Angelo, not to save her brother; indeed in her first revulsion, when he begs for his life she says " 'tis best that thou diest quickly." Almost at the end of the play, the Duke tells her that he could have saved her brother but acted with "slower foot," apparently because he wanted some more fun with his plot; but after all Claudio is better dead: "That life is better life, past fearing death, Than one that lives to fear. Make it your comfort, So happy is your brother." "I do, my lord," is the brisk and hearty answer. Here, by the way, we find Bradley's principle, that the characters are better dead, in full command of the stage; Angelo in his turn "craves death more willingly than mercy." But Isabella does not apply it to Angelo. We are given a further test of the quality of her feeling, in the appeal of Mariana for his life. She does react with the mercy enjoined by her religion, and this is certainly meant to be to her credit, but she attains this height by an impulse of personal vanity so repulsive as to surprise even Dr. Johnson.

> I partly think,
> A due sincerity govern'd his deeds
> Till he did look on me.   (v.1.448)

She knows the history of Mariana, who is appealing for Angelo's life beside her; in fact the Duke has told her that when Mariana lost most of her marriage portion Angelo "swallowed his vows whole, pretending in her discoveries of dishonour." Afterwards, when Isabella's brother is presented to her still alive, she does not speak to him at all; no doubt the plot gave no room for a long speech, but the Bard is not as tonguetied as all that if he can think of anything for a character to say. The apologists have objected that flippant modern critics merely do not understand the old reverence for virginity if they dwell on such points. But it is impossible to suppose all these details are accidental; they are not even clumsy; they are pointed. It seems to me the only working theory to suppose that Shakespeare could not quite stomach the old reverence either.

And on this view the final use of *sense* can carry a good deal of meaning, though if you suppose the Duke meant all of it he is not likely to have married her afterwards. "Against all reason"—"all normal decent feeling"—"all depth or delicacy of feeling"; whatever kind of *sense* is meant here, she lacks it. For a moment, in the elaborate and teasing balance of the play, Shakespeare turns even against mercy, or at least against the abstract rule of mercy from which she acts. She is too otherworldly to feel the thing like a sane person; she is not sensual enough, the word might argue, to have tolerable human feelings.

This is certainly not what the Duke thinks; here as always, however savagely he tests her, he finds her ideally right. If

he means any irony in the word, apart
from the general triumph in knowing better than his audience which he is enjoying
in all these uses of *sense*, it is that she is
altogther above "sense," above the whole
view of life which even a good use of the
suggestions of the word would imply. Miss
M. C. Bradbrook, in an essay on the play
(*Review of English Studies* XVII.385), has
maintained that the Duke did not expect
Isabel to forgive Angelo, but accepts her
superior wisdom when "her justice recognises the one grain of good in him." I am
not sure how much a verbal analysis can
prove, and I would think this view wrong
without one, but surely those who support
it must find it less plausible when they notice that this use of the word is the last of
a series of uses by the Duke in this scene,
and that the previous ones (whatever else
they mean) have all carried secret boasts
of superior knowledge. It does not seem to
me that there was any subtle unconscious-
ness about the matter; I think Shakespeare
felt he was "polishing off" the series of
puns on *sense* by this very dramatic final
use of it. But if he meant to kick away his
key word at the end, it seems to me, he
could not manage to do it. This is not to
say that he took the same cheery view of
the affair as Lucio; the play repeatedly
tells us that Lucio took venereal disease for
granted, and I think this practical argument gave the basic emotional drive in favour of purity. Claudio ends the old story
with a brave and generous action, giving
himself up in the expectation of death to
save the life of Angelo, now married to his
sister; Shakespeare would not allow him so
much dignity, and altered the plot. This
seems good evidence that he found the behaviour of Claudio disgusting. But he
could not convince himself, it seems to me,
even that the Duke was agreeable, let alone
that Isabella was. The pomposity of the
man he probably found natural, but the
touchiness, the confidence in error, the self-
indulgence of his incessant lying, must I
think always have been absurd.

Various critics during this century have
tried to show that Shakespeare in his heart
disliked his pompous old men, Prospero for
example, and merely assumed that the audience would put up with them sufficiently to
make the mechanics of the play tolerable.
On the other hand Mr. Wilson Knight, who
is highminded and warmhearted in a rather Victorian manner, tends to make these
old men into practically undiluted symbols
of heavenly virtue. The Duke raises this
problem particularly sharply, and I should
not agree that the problem is for some logical reason inherently unreal ("if we dig into the picture we only go through the can-
vas"); surely any producer has to make up
his mind about it. Mr. Wilson Knight considers that:

> The Duke's ethic is born of his knowledge of
> good and evil potential in himself. And his re-
> membrance of his own evil, which is crucial to his
> ethic, is kept alive by Lucio's chattering of his
> supposed vices at his side. Lucio causes the Duke
> to distrust the ideal of purity in Isabella by con-
> tinually suggesting that such an ideal is a form
> of insincerity. Iago causes Othello to distrust his
> ideal of purity by suggesting its impurity; the two
> triangles may thus be shown to bear a close re-
> semblance to each other.

I think this parallel is a searching one, but
I do not see that the text gives us any en-
couragement (apart from one very obscure
piece of doggerel closing the third act, in
which the unreal style lets the Duke act as
a sort of chorus) for ascribing to the Duke
an idea about ethics which is simply the
playwright's. Mr. Wilson Knight seems to
regard as important evidence the Duke's
remarks about not liking to stage himself
before the people's eyes (the idea comes in
twice, but he stages himself very elaborate-
ly at the end of the play). The same feelings had been expressed by James I, to
the annoyance of the public, and the audience might well notice the resemblance;
this is an argument against supposing that
the Duke was frankly ridiculed in performance, because it might be dangerous, but

Shakespeare could not assume that everybody would interpret the foibles of James as a proof of a high and selfless view of ethics. In any case, the higher you pitch the ethics of the Duke, the more surprising you must find his behaviour.

It seems hard not to regard him as a comic character. Indeed the play gives us a sufficiently memorable phrase to sum him up; he is "the old fantastical Duke of Dark Corners." In the fourth scene the Friar points out that, if the Duke defends the revival of the old law by Angelo, he should have revived it himself; that would have been more impressive. The Duke replies:

> I do fear, too dreadful:
> Sith 'twas my fault to give the people scope
> 'Twould be my tyranny to strike and gall them
> For what I bid them do. . . . Therefore indeed, my father,
> I have on Angelo imposed the office
> Who may, in the ambush of my name, strike home
> And yet my nature never in the sight
> To do it slander.

To be sure, he seems to be lying as usual; we heard him specifically tell Angelo "Your scope is as mine own, So to enforce or qualify the laws. As to your soul seems good"; and he goes on to tell the Friar that he is testing Angelo. But surely on the stage this excuse is too prominent to be forgotten, and the combination of vanity and cowardice cannot be intended for praise. It does have a note of puritanical self-examination, as Mr. Knight would claim, but I would not call that enough to give it a high spiritual ethic. No doubt it could be carried off by grandeur of manner; but when the Duke buzzes from Claudio to Isabella, all agog, and busily telling lies to both, I do not see how the author can be banking on the simple-minded respect of the audience for great persons. The subtlety of his justice has been praised, and indeed there is a curious passage where he claims that all his prisoners are either executed or released. But he is asking why Barnadine had been kept in jail seven years; the excuse of the provost is that "his friends still wrought reprieves for him" while there was no proof adequate to kill him on. What the Duke urges Mariana to do ("He is your husband on a pre-contract; To bring you thus together is no sin") can only be distinguished, if at all, by a technicality from what Claudio is to be killed for doing ("she is fast my wife Save that we do the denunciation lack Of outward order; this we came not to, Only for propagation of a dower"); and the Duke apparently approves of the law which would kill Claudio, at least he tells the Friar that he does, at considerable length. Incidentally this law would also have killed Shakespeare, whose first child was born soon after marriage; his distaste for lust at the time of writing did not (I take it) carry him so far as to make him agree with the Duke here.

But perhaps all this is picking holes. What makes the Duke ridiculous on the stage is the fuss he makes about the backbiting of Lucio, that is, precisely what makes Mr. Knight think him so high and pure. The Duke of course is in disguise when Lucio tells him these things, and he answers by boasting about himself, in a phrase which seems an obvious dramatic irony, "let him but be testimonied in his own bringing forth, and he shall appear to the envious a scholar, a statesman and a soldier." He anxiously questions Escalus in the hope of hearing something better, and continues to drag the subject up when we are thinking about the plot. The soliloquy "Oh place and greatness" (iv.1.60), while Isabella is trying to induce Mariana to play her part, is so much out of key that at first we think he is talking about Angelo. In the final scene, the mutual petty accusations of Lucio and the Duke, working up to "yet here's one in place I cannot pardon," are good farce and nothing else. No doubt there was a casualness and good-humour about the Elizabethan stage, so that the great man could be laughed at for a bit and resume greatness when required; but this is only to say that there was room for

Shakespeare to put in mixed feelings of his own.

But it is true, I think, that there is an agreeable side of the Duke; it becomes dramatically prominent on the occasions when he is proved absurdly wrong. He is certain (iv. III) that Angelo will be sending a pardon for Claudio to the prison (thinking he has enjoyed Isabella); and he keeps boasting to the provost of his superior knowledge. When the letter is opened it orders an earlier execution under cover of night. The Duke immediately starts plotting again, apparently unperturbed, but the fact that he could not imagine the depth of evil that he is playing with does, I think, operate on us as somehow to his credit. From then on his tricks seem less offensive; the claim to divine foreknowledge has been broken. Also by this time it has become clear that nothing less than the fantastic behaviour of the Duke could have kept the play from being a tragedy. The whole force of the case against Angelo is that, in the ordinary way, he would have been completely safe; he is a symbol of justice itself, as Escalus points out (iii. II, end); he can only be imagined as vulnerable if he is handled by very strange means. In the same way the Duke's final test of Isabella, that she must forgive Angelo still believing he killed her brother treacherously, is a result of his general expectation of mercy; the fact that she agrees to it for bad reasons is not one that he is likely to realise. One might even find it pathetic that the intended nun should say "I partly think A due sincerity governed his deeds Till he did look on me." Her new sensual vanity seems meant to imply a partial awakening of her senses after the battering she has gone through; and her decision to marry the Duke is perhaps not so grossly out of character as critics have supposed.

What is really offensive about the Duke is the other side of this quality which can be found agreeable; it is offensive, I mean, that he should treat his subjects as puppets for the fun of making them twitch. But here, I suppose, the Character is saved by the Plot. It seems a peculiarly brutal flippancy that he should not only trick Isabella about Claudio unnecessarily but take pains to thrust the imagined death of Claudio upon her mind. His moral claims about it—

> But I will keep her ignorant of her good
> To make her heavenly comforts of despair

—do not seem to me tolerable even on Bradley's principle; he is playing at being God. But there is a question here of the mechanics of working on an audience; we forgive him for it because Isabella turns out not to care a rap about Claudio, and we wanted to know whether she would. The reasons why it seems all right, if you followed them up, would lead to quite a different view of the story.

And yet I think the play is a whole in spite of this chasm in one's view of the two good characters; even if Shakespeare was only grumbling to himself about them, an audience could share his feelings without ruining the performance. The Duke's flippancy about justice corresponds to a deeper and more desperate feeling in the author, elaborated throughout the action and insisted upon in the title, that the whole business of public justice is fatuous and hideous, whether compared to the mercy of Christ or the humanity of private life. There is an echo of the same idea when Pompey shifts over comfortably from a bawd to a hangman. Mr. Wilson Knight was quite right to feel that there is a subtle ethic in the play somewhere, and that it is mixed up with Christianity. But I think there is a balancing idea to this, one that accounts for the unpleasantness of the two good characters. It is perhaps simply the idea that one must not act on these absolutes prematurely. Even granting that the conditions of life are inherently repulsive, a man makes himself actually more repulsive by acting on this truth; you cannot get outside the world and above justice, and a ruler who sets out to do this (except under very peculiar circumstances, by luck) is merely bad at his job. And the same ambivalence clings to the divine Isabella. In a way, indeed, I think this is a complete and successful work of the master, but the way is a very odd one, because it amounts to pretending to write a romantic comedy and in fact keeping the audience's teeth slightly but increasingly on edge. And on this view, I should claim, the performance with the word *sense* is made to echo the thought of the play very fully up to the end. . . .